a
jane austen
education

HOW SIX NOVELS TAUGHT ME
ABOUT LOVE, FRIENDSHIP, AND THE
THINGS THAT REALLY MATTER

also by william deresiewicz

Jane Austen and the Romantic Poets

a
jane austen
education

HOW SIX NOVELS TAUGHT ME
ABOUT LOVE, FRIENDSHIP, AND THE
THINGS THAT REALLY MATTER

WILLIAM DERESIEWICZ

THE PENGUIN PRESS

New York

2011

THE PENGUIN PRESS
Published by the Penguin Group
Penguin Group (USA) Inc., 375 Hudson Street, New York, New York 10014, U.S.A. • Penguin
Group (Canada), 90 Eglinton Avenue East, Suite 700, Toronto, Ontario, Canada M4P 2Y3
(a division of Pearson Penguin Canada Inc.) • Penguin Books Ltd, 80 Strand, London
WC2R 0RL, England • Penguin Ireland, 25 St. Stephen's Green, Dublin 2, Ireland (a division
of Penguin Books Ltd) • Penguin Books Australia Ltd, 250 Camberwell Road, Camberwell,
Victoria 3124, Australia (a division of Pearson Australia Group Pty Ltd) • Penguin Books
India Pvt Ltd, 11 Community Centre, Panchsheel Park, New Delhi – 110 017, India • Penguin
Group (NZ), 67 Apollo Drive, Rosedale, Auckland 0632, New Zealand (a division of Pearson
New Zealand Ltd) • Penguin Books (South Africa) (Pty) Ltd, 24 Sturdee Avenue, Rosebank,
Johannesburg 2196, South Africa

Penguin Books Ltd, Registered Offices: 80 Strand, London WC2R 0RL, England

First published in 2011 by The Penguin Press, a member of Penguin Group (USA) Inc.

LIBRARY OF CONGRESS CATALOGING IN PUBLICATION DATA
Deresiewicz, William.
A Jane Austen education : how six novels taught me about love, friendship, and the things
that really matter / William Deresiewicz.
p.   cm.
ISBN 978-1-59420-288-9
1. Austen, Jane, 1775-1817—Appreciation.   I. Title.
PR4037.D47   2011   2010045828
823'.7—dc22

Printed in the United States of America

1   3   5   7   9   10   8   6   4   2

DESIGNED BY NICOLE LAROCHE

To Jill,

and to the memory of Karl Kroeber

contents

a
jane austen
education

HOW SIX NOVELS TAUGHT ME
ABOUT LOVE, FRIENDSHIP, AND THE
THINGS THAT REALLY MATTER

CHAPTER 1

emma
everyday matters

I was twenty-six, and about as dumb, in all human things, as any twenty-six-year-old has a right to be, when I met the woman who would change my life. That she'd been dead for a couple of hundred years made not the slightest difference whatsoever. Her name was Jane Austen, and she would teach me everything I know about everything that matters.

The thing that takes my breath away when I think back on it all is that I never wanted to read her in the first place. It happened quite by accident, and very much against my will. I had been eager, when I'd gone back to school to get my Ph.D. the year before, to fill the gaps in my literary education—Chaucer and Shakespeare, Melville and Milton—but the one area of English literature that held no interest for me, that positively repelled me, was nineteenth-century British fiction. What could be duller, I thought, than a bunch of long, heavy novels, by women novelists, in stilted language, on trivial subjects?

The very titles sounded ridiculous. *Jane Eyre. Wuthering Heights. Middlemarch.* But nothing symbolized the dullness and narrowness of that whole body of work like the name Jane Austen. Wasn't she the one who wrote those silly romantic fairy tales? Just thinking about her made me sleepy.

What I really wanted to study was modernism, the literature that had formed my identity as a reader and, in many ways, as a person. Joyce, Conrad, Faulkner, Nabokov: complex, difficult, sophisticated works. Like so many young men, I needed to think of myself as a rebel, and modernism, with its revolutionary intensity, confirmed my self-image. I'd pass my days in a cloud of angry sarcasm, making silent speeches, as I stalked down Broadway in my John Lennon coat, against everything conventional, respectable, and pious. I'd walk right up alongside the buildings, in the shadows—it makes you feel like a rat scuttling for cover—to aggravate my sense of alienation. If I was waiting for someone and had nowhere else to go, I'd sit right down on the sidewalk with my Kerouac or my *Catch-22*, just you try and stop me. I smoked weed, listened to the Clash, and snorted at the business monkeys who'd sold out to the Man. Like the modernists, I was hot to change the world, even if I wasn't sure exactly how. At the very least, I knew I wasn't going to let the world change me. I was Dostoyevsky's Underground Man, raging against the machine. I was Joyce's Stephen Dedalus, the rebel artist who runs rings around the grownups. I was Conrad's Marlow, the world-weary truth teller who punches through hypocrisy and lies.

Needless to say, I was not the easiest person to get along with. In fact, I wonder that my friends put up with me at all. Like so many guys, I thought that a good conversation meant holding forth about all the supposedly important things I knew: books, history, politics, whatever. But I wasn't just aggressively certain of myself—though of course I never let anyone finish a sentence and delivered my opinions as if they'd come direct from Sinai. I was also oblivious to the feelings of the people around me, a bulldozer stuck in overdrive, because it had never occurred to me to imagine how things might look from someone else's point of view.

My best friend, who knew me better than I knew myself, once introduced me to a friend of hers named Honour. Just as I was gearing up to reel off all the stupid puns I could think of—"Your Honor," "Honored to meet you," and so forth—my friend caught the smirk spreading across my face and cut me off before I could make an idiot of myself. "Billy," she explained with the weary patience with which you might address a difficult child, "she's already heard them all." Basically, I had no insight into myself or anyone else.

My romantic life, not surprisingly, had never been particularly happy. I was stuck at the time in a relationship that should have ended long before. We had jumped each other one night the previous summer, and though we'd been together for over a year, we had little in common and had never much progressed beyond the sex. She was gorgeous, bisexual, impulsive, experienced, with a look that knew things and a laugh that didn't give a damn. We would go to bed, and then we would go dancing, and then we would go to bed again.

But as for anything like real intimacy, I just couldn't manage it. I'd had girlfriends before, including ones I'd even thought I'd loved, but things had always ended badly: fights, sulks, head games, tears. Eventually, good riddance. At least this time we didn't fight. We didn't talk, either—not about anything real, not about what was going on with us or what we might have been feeling. Instead, I'd hold forth as usual, even think I was doing her a favor in the process. I was a graduate student at Columbia, after all, and she had barely scraped through college. I was going to do something important with my life, and she was marking time as a waitress—a job that struck me as depressingly unambitious—while she tried to figure out her next move. In short, I didn't respect her enough to imagine that she might have anything to say to me that was worth listening to.

I knew it wasn't a real relationship, but I kept telling myself that this was what I'd always wanted. A steady supply of sex, with no strings attached: a teenage boy's idea of paradise. Except I wasn't a teenage boy anymore. Still, I thought—and this is how numb I was by then—well, so maybe I never will find that one person to love. So what? I knew, deep down, that the idea of doing without love for the rest of my life was completely absurd, that it was a sign of grave emotional peril that it could even occur to me, but I managed to keep the lid on my denial. Besides, I thought, as soon as you fell in love, people started expecting you to get married. And if there was one thing I knew, it was that I was never going to get married.

．　．　．

My second year in graduate school, I signed up for a class called Studies in the Novel, less because I knew anything about it than because it sounded like a good fit. Our first two books were *Madame Bovary,* the novel that raised the art of fiction to a new level of cultural esteem, and *The Ambassadors,* Henry James's most honored masterpiece. So far, my need to study prestigious literature was being satisfied.

Then came *Emma.* I had heard some scattered talk, over the years, about its supposed greatness—one of the best novels in the language, more complex than anything in Joyce or Proust—but at first, my prejudices against Jane Austen were only confirmed. Everything was so unbearably banal. The story seemed to consist of nothing more than a lot of chitchat among a bunch of commonplace characters in a country village. No grand events, no great issues, and, inexplicably for a writer of romance novels, not even any passion.

Emma, it turned out, was Emma Woodhouse, "handsome, clever, and rich," who lived with her feeble, foolish old father on their family estate of Hartfield. Her life was impossibly narrow. Her mother had died when she was a baby; her sister, Isabella, lived in London; and the governess who had raised her had just gotten married. Mr. Woodhouse himself was too much of a hypochondriac to even venture off the estate, and his best friends, who were forever dropping by, consisted of a sad, silly spinster named Miss Bates and her elderly mother, the widow of the old clergyman.

This was a pretty unpromising bunch of people to begin with, and then all they seemed to do was sit around and *talk*: about who was sick, who had had a card party the night before, who had said what to whom. Mr. Woodhouse's idea of a big time was taking a stroll around the garden. Reading the mail was the highlight of everybody's day, and a shopping trip to Highbury, the little village near Hartfield where the Bateses lived—and where there seemed to be a total of one store—counted for the heroine as a major event.

I couldn't believe how trivial this all was. In my other classes, D. H. Lawrence was preaching sexual revolution and Norman Mailer was cursing his way through World War II, and here I was reading about card parties. One whole chapter—Isabella had just brought her family home for Christmas—consisted entirely of aimless talk, as everyone caught up on one another's news. For more than half a dozen pages, the plot simply came to a halt. But the truth was, for long stretches of the book there really wasn't much plot to speak of. Things happened, story lines developed, but no single issue, no point of suspense, moved the story forward—especially not the one I'd been led to expect, the one about the heroine's romantic future, which the book hardly even seemed to address.

What was the point of all those long, rambling speeches by Emma's father? Here he was, talking to Emma about Isabella's sons:

> *Henry is a fine boy, but John is very like his mama. Henry is the eldest, he was named after me, not after his father. John, the second, is named after his father. Some people are sur-*

prised, I believe, that the eldest was not, but Isabella would have him called Henry, which I thought very pretty of her. And he is a very clever boy, indeed. They are all remarkably clever; and they have so many pretty ways. They will come and stand by my chair, and say, "Grandpapa, can you give me a bit of string?" and once Henry asked me for a knife, but I told him knives were only made for grandpapas.

Emma undoubtedly knew all this, had heard it a hundred times. The information wasn't for our benefit, either. The boys, their cleverness, and their desire for knives and string played no role whatsoever in the story. And we knew by then that Emma's father was a tedious old man. So why did we have to listen to this?

Mr. Woodhouse, what was more, was nothing compared to Miss Bates. He driveled by the paragraph; she prosed by the page. I'd be sitting in a coffee shop, surrounded by people reading Kierkegaard or Chomsky, and get to a paragraph like this, where she told Emma about a letter she had just received from her niece, Jane Fairfax. Or tried to, anyway:

Oh! here it is. I was sure it could not be far off; but I had put my huswife upon it, you see, without being aware, and so it was quite hid, but I had it in my hand so very lately that I was almost sure it must be on the table. I was reading it to Mrs. Cole, and since she went away, I was reading it again to my mother, for it is such a pleasure to her—a letter from Jane—that she can never hear it often enough; so I knew it could not be far off, and here it is, only just under my huswife—and since you are so kind as to wish to hear what she says;—but, first of all, I really must, in justice to Jane, apologize for her writing so short a letter—only two pages you see—hardly two—and in general she fills the whole paper and crosses half. . . .

And that was only the first part of the speech, and we didn't get to hear what the letter actually said for another page after that.

Mr. Woodhouse and Miss Bates—the dull old man, the scatterbrained neighbor—were the kind of people I tuned out in real life. I'd stare past them and hurry on my way, or nod absentmindedly and think about how I needed to get my library books renewed. I certainly didn't want to spend my time reading about them.

The funny thing was, the heroine agreed with me. If I was bored with Highbury, so was Emma. She didn't think that anything interesting was going on there either, and what little plot the novel had involved her determination to get things moving on her own. I wasn't sure how I felt about this. On the one hand, I sympathized with her. On the other, she went about everything so blindly and willfully, and all her schemes turned out to be such disasters, that I found myself cringing almost every time she opened her mouth.

Early on, casting about for something to do, Emma struck up a friendship with a girl named Harriet Smith. Harriet was docile, ignorant, and naïve—a worshipful younger friend who flattered Emma's vanity in every way. She was also very pretty—

"short, plump, and fair, with a fine bloom, blue eyes, light hair, and a look of great sweetness"—and that gave Emma an idea. "Those soft blue eyes, and all those natural graces," she thought, "should not be wasted." Harriet "wanted only a little more knowledge and elegance to be quite perfect." And so, like Henry Higgins sizing up Eliza Doolittle, Emma decided to turn her friend into a project. "She would improve her . . . and introduce her into good society; she would form her opinions and her manners. It would be an interesting, and certainly a very kind undertaking; highly becoming her own situation in life."

This was really too much. Such arrogance, such nosiness— and from someone who was all of twenty herself, and scarcely less naïve than her friend. Emma gave herself credit for bringing about her governess's marriage with a local gentleman—though all she'd really done was guess that it would happen—and now she set about arranging a match for Harriet with Mr. Elton, the new clergyman. The idea was ridiculous—Harriet was the illegitimate daughter of an unknown father, with no money or social standing—but Emma convinced herself otherwise.

Worse, she convinced her friend, persuading Harriet to turn down a proposal from a worthy young farmer, Mr. Martin, whom Harriet liked very much. The scene was excruciating, like watching someone torture a puppy:

> *"You think I ought to refuse him then," said Harriet, looking down.*
>
> *"Ought to refuse him! My dear Harriet, what do you mean? Are you in any doubt as to that? I thought—but I beg your pardon, perhaps I have been under a mistake. I cer-*

*tainly have been misunderstanding you, if you feel in doubt
as to the* purport *of your answer. I had imagined you were
consulting me only as to the wording of it."*

*Harriet was silent. With a little reserve of manner, Emma
continued:*

"You mean to return a favourable answer, I collect."

*"No, I do not; that is, I do not mean—What shall I do?
What would you advise me to do? Pray, dear Miss Woodhouse, tell me what I ought to do."* . . .

*"Not for the world," said Emma, smiling graciously,
"would I advise you either way."*

Now I really couldn't stand her. To play with someone else's
happiness, whether she knew it or not, simply for the sake of
her own vanity! Just as Emma thought that no one in Highbury
was good enough for her, so did she think that Mr. Martin
wasn't good enough for her friend—not because she thought
so much of Harriet, but just because she was *her* friend. In the
same way, she knew that Miss Bates and her mother were lonely
women, teetering on the edge of poverty, and that a visit from
her always made their day, but she could never bring herself to
drop by as often as she knew she should, and when she did show
up, she would find an excuse to run away as fast as possible.
Jane Fairfax, Miss Bates's niece, was an intelligent, talented,
gracious young woman, right around the heroine's age, who
came to Highbury for a couple of months every year—but
Emma did all she could to avoid her. Any relative of the lowly
Miss Bates, after all, could hardly be a suitable companion for
the great Emma Woodhouse.

Eventually, Emma's bored disdain for the people around her led her to her very worst moment. Frank Churchill, her governess's stepson, had come to Highbury for a visit. Frank was lively, good-looking, a little bit of a bad boy, and he played up to Emma so extravagantly that her head grew bigger than ever. It was summer, and they all decided to go on a picnic: Emma, Frank, Harriet, Jane Fairfax, Miss Bates, Mr. Elton—everyone who mattered. When they actually got there, though, Emma and Frank's flirtation was so oppressive to everybody else that they all soon found themselves sitting around with nothing to say. So Frank devised a happy plan to have them entertain the grand young lady. "Here are seven of you," he announced, "and she only demands from each of you either one thing very clever, . . . or two things moderately clever, . . . or three things very dull indeed." Poor, harmless Miss Bates, who knew perfectly well how tedious everybody found her, was left feeling very self-conscious. "Oh! very well," she exclaimed, "then I need not be uneasy. 'Three things very dull indeed.' That will just do for me, you know. I shall be sure to say three dull things as soon as ever I open my mouth, shan't I?"

And that was when Emma, carried away by Frank's flattery and her own sense of effortless superiority, hit bottom. "Ah! ma'am, but there may be a difficulty. Pardon me—but you will be limited as to number—only three at once." It was a shocking piece of cruelty, all the worse for the way that its victim received it:

Miss Bates, deceived by the mock ceremony of her manner, did not immediately catch her meaning; but, when it burst

on her, it could not anger, though a slight blush shewed that
it could pain her.

   "Ah!—well—to be sure. Yes, I see what she means, . . . and
I will try to hold my tongue. I must make myself very dis-
agreeable, or she would not have said such a thing to an old
friend."

And that was when I finally understood what Austen had been
up to all along. Emma's cruelty, which I was so quick to criti-
cize, was nothing, I saw, but the mirror image of my own. The
boredom and contempt that the book aroused were not signs
of Austen's ineptitude; they were the exact responses she
wanted me to have. She had incited them, in order to expose
them. By creating a heroine who felt exactly as I did, and who
behaved precisely as I would have in her situation, she was
showing me my own ugly face. I couldn't deplore Emma's disdain for Miss Bates, or her boredom with the whole commonplace Highbury world, without simultaneously condemning
my own.

   Austen, I realized, had not been writing about everyday
things because she couldn't think of anything else to talk about.
She had been writing about them because she wanted to show
how important they really are. All that trivia hadn't been marking time until she got to the point. It *was* the point. Austen
wasn't silly and superficial; she was much, much smarter—and
much wiser—than I could ever have imagined.

   I returned to the novel in a completely different frame of
mind. Mr. Woodhouse's banalities, Miss Bates's monologues,
all that gossip and small talk—Austen put them in as a sign that

she respected her characters, not because she wanted us to look down on them. She was willing to listen to what they had to say, and she wanted me to listen, too. As long as I had treated such passages as filler and hurried through them, they had seemed impossibly dull. But once I started to slow down long enough to take them on their own terms, I found that they possessed their own gravity, their own dignity, their own sweetness.

Jane Fairfax's letters and where they may have been hiding, little John and Henry's cleverness and pretty ways—these things mattered, because they mattered to the characters themselves. They made up the texture of their lives, and gave their existence its savor. I got it now. By eliminating all the big, noisy events that usually absorb our interest when we read novels— the adventures and affairs, the romances and the crises, even, at times, the plot—Austen was asking us to pay attention to the things we usually miss or don't accord enough esteem, in novels or in life. Those small, "trivial," everyday things, the things that happen hour by hour to the people in our lives: what your nephew said, what your friend heard, what your neighbor did. That, she was telling us, is what the fabric of our years really consists of. That is what life is really about.

Even Emma knew this. She just didn't know she knew it. "There was not a creature in the world," Austen wrote about her governess, Mrs. Weston, to whom the heroine spoke "with such unreserve":

> not any one, to whom she related with such conviction of being listened to and understood, of being always interesting and always intelligible, the little affairs, arrangements,

perplexities, and pleasures of her father and herself. She could tell nothing of Hartfield, in which Mrs. Weston had not a lively concern; and half an hour's uninterrupted communication of all those little matters on which the daily happiness of private life depends, was one of the first gratifications of each.

Emma was always looking in the wrong direction. Her heart was in the right place—that was what ultimately made me forgive her, and, finally, what saved her—but her busy brain led her astray. While she plotted her schemes and dreamed her dreams, her "daily happiness" was right there in front of her, in "affairs, arrangements, perplexities, and pleasures"—the hourly ordinary, in all its granular specificity.

The novel had a name for this gossipy texture of daily life, a word I stumbled upon again and again. "Many little particulars"; "I am impatient for a thousand particulars"; "She will give you all the minute particulars." Not just particulars, but "little" particulars, "minute" particulars. Life is lived at the level of the little. In fact, I now saw, it was remarkable just how many things in the novel were "little." "Little particulars." "Little affairs, arrangements, perplexities, and pleasures." Harriet Smith was "little," always. Her friends the Martins had "a little Welch cow, a very pretty little Welch cow," and a little gazebo in the garden, just big enough to hold a dozen people. The story took place entirely within the vicinity of Highbury, and space itself seemed contracted by the smallness of the frame. The distance between Emma's house and Mrs. Weston's was only half a mile, yet it was made to seem like an arduous journey. Though *Emma* was over four hundred pages long, its whole scale was little, like a crowded scene inscribed upon a miniature.

If I was having trouble seeing the importance of the world that Austen was putting in front of me, in other words, it wasn't entirely my fault. Like all the great teachers, I now saw, she made us come to her. She had momentous truths to tell, but she concealed them in humble packages. Her "littleness" was really an optical illusion, a test. Jesus spoke in parables so his disciples would have to make an effort to understand him. The truth, he knew, cannot be grasped in any other way. Austen reminded me, I realized, of something that Plato said about his great mentor Socrates, who also taught by telling stories. "His words are ridiculous when you first hear them, for his talk is of pack-asses and smiths and cobblers . . . so that any ignorant or inexperienced person might feel disposed to laugh at him; but he who sees what is within will find that they are the only words which have a meaning in them, and likewise the most divine."

Austen's words, quite apart from what she said with them, also struck me as ridiculous when I first heard them. I was used to stylistic brilliance that hit you over the head: Joyce's syntactic labyrinths, Nabokov's arcane vocabulary, Hemingway's bleached-bone austerities. So what was I supposed to make of passages like this, near the start of the novel?

Mr. Woodhouse was fond of society in his own way. He liked very much to have his friends come and see him; and

from various united causes, from his long residence at Hart-
field, and his good nature, from his fortune, his house, and
his daughter, he could command the visits of his own little
circle, in a great measure, as he liked. He had not much in-
tercourse with any families beyond that circle; his horror of
late hours, and large dinner-parties, made him unfit for any
acquaintance but such as would visit him on his own terms.

No metaphors, no images, no flights of lyricism. This hardly
seemed like writing at all. Aside from the slightly dated vocabulary, it was more like talking.

But then I started to look more carefully. Mr. Woodhouse
was, in the language of Austen's day, a valetudinarian, or sort
of professional invalid. No one seemed weaker, no one more
powerless. And yet in just three sentences, by the subtlest of
means, Austen established him as a man who used that weak-
ness to control the world around him. There were fewer than a
hundred words in that passage, and fully seventeen, nearly one
in five, were pronouns that referred to him: "he," "him," "his."
"His" fortune, "his" house, "his" daughter—everything, as it
were, was "his." The passage started with his name, and his
power was affirmed at the end of every sentence. He did things
"in his own way," "as he liked," and "on his own terms."

This, I now saw, was how all of Austen's language worked.
No strain, no display, no effort to awe or impress. Just everyday
words in their natural order—a language that didn't call attention to itself in any way, but just rolled along as easily as breathing. It wasn't the words that Austen used that created her
effects, it was the way she used them, the way she grouped and

balanced them. And so it was, I saw, with her characters. A thousand authors could write novels about ordinary people, but only one of those books would be *Emma*. Austen's characters came to seem so vivid, so meaningful, because she put them down on the page exactly the way she placed her words: without condescension, without apology, but with a masterful talent for arrangement. Emma was balanced by Jane Fairfax, and Miss Bates by Harriet Smith, and Mr. Martin by Mr. Elton, and all of them by one another, setting the whole story in motion and creating scenes that felt as natural as real life. It didn't matter how small the frame was, because it contained a whole world.

As it turned out, people had been reacting to Jane Austen exactly as I had for as long as they'd been reading her. The first reviews warned that readers might find her stories "trifling," with "no great variety," "extremely deficient" in imagination and "entirely devoid of invention," with "so little narrative" that it was hard to even describe what they were about. Austen herself, who liked to collect her friends' and family's opinions of her books, recorded that a certain Mrs. Guiton found *Emma* "too natural to be interesting." Madame de Staël, an illustrious French intellectual, thought her work "*vulgaire*"—which makes it just as well that Austen declined to meet her formidable contemporary at a London dinner party when she had the chance.

Austen knew that she wasn't creating for just anybody. "I do not write for such dull Elves," she said of *Pride and Prejudice*, adapting some lines of poetry, "As have not a great deal of Ingenuity themselves." And *Emma,* she knew, would be the hardest challenge of all. "I am going to take a heroine," she said as she was about to start working on the novel, "whom no-one but myself will much like."

But from the beginning, there were readers of discernment who recognized her genius behind the façade. No less a judge than Sir Walter Scott, the leading writer of her day, author of epic poems and sweeping historical novels like *Ivanhoe* and *The Bride of Lammermoor,* confessed her superiority:

> *That young lady had a talent for describing the involvements and feelings and characters of ordinary life which is to me the most wonderful I ever met with. The Big Bow-wow strain I can do myself like any now going; but the exquisite touch, which renders ordinary commonplace things and characters interesting, from the truth of description and sentiment, is denied me.*

Another critic poked fun at readers who thought that there could be but "little merit in making characters act and talk so exactly like the people whom they saw around them every day," not recognizing that, as with Mozart or Rembrandt, the highest art lies in concealing art. Such readers, he joked, were like the man who couldn't see why everyone was making a big fuss about a certain celebrated actor, "who merely behaved on the stage as anybody might be expected to in real life."

Her reputation slowly grew, but by the late 1800s there were only two opinions about Jane Austen. Either you loved her or you hated her. Mark Twain, a famously exuberant hater, swore that reading Austen made him feel "like a barkeep entering the kingdom of heaven." "It seems a great pity to me," he taunted an Austen fan, "that they allowed her to die a natural death." "Every time I read *Pride and Prejudice*," he told another friend, "I want to dig her up and hit her over the skull with her own shinbone."

But if you loved her—if you "got" her—you felt like you'd joined a secret club, with its own code words and special signs and degrees of initiation. It was a creed, in the words of one writer, "as ardent as a religion," and "a real appreciation of *Emma*," her subtlest book of all, was "the final test of citizenship in her kingdom." Rudyard Kipling, very much a citizen himself, celebrated the phenomenon in "The Janeites," a story about Austen worship in, of all places, the trenches of World War I. "Jane?" says Humberstall, the simple-minded veteran at the heart of the story—

> *Why, she was a little old maid 'oo'd written 'alf a dozen books about a hundred years ago. 'Twasn't as if there was anythin' to them, either. I know. I had to read 'em. They weren't adventurous, nor smutty, nor what you'd call even interestin'—all about girls o' seventeen . . . , not certain 'oom they'd like to marry; an' their dances an' card-parties an' picnics, and their young blokes goin' off to London on 'orseback for 'air-cuts an' shaves.* [Which is exactly what Frank Churchill does in *Emma*.]

Yet once Humberstall was accepted into the brotherhood— "it's a very select Society, an' you've got to be a Janeite in your 'eart"—he came to understand her true worth. "I read all her six books now for pleasure 'tween times in the shop. . . . You take it from me, Brethren, there's no one to touch Jane when you're in a tight place. Gawd bless 'er, whoever she was."

The very first review of *Emma* was written by none other than Sir Walter Scott himself. If people had trouble recogniz- ing the value of the novel's portrait of daily life, he said, if they thought of it as a book in which "nothing happened," that's be- cause they were so used to reading novels in which all too *many* things happened. Austen lived in the great age of trash fiction: the gothic novel, the sentimental novel, the bodice ripper— crumbling castles, creaking doors, and secret passageways; heavenly maidens and dark seducers, piercing shrieks and floods of tears, wild rides and breathless escapes; shipwrecks, death- beds, abductions, avowals; poverty, misery, rape, and incest. And of course, at the last minute, by grace of the author and a heap of coincidences, a happy ending.

Austen herself made delirious fun of this kind of nonsense when she was young. Her juvenilia—the satirical skits and sketches she produced as a girl for the entertainment of her large, literate, fun-loving family, some of which were written when she was no more than twelve—are full of wicked paro- dies of this fashionable fluff. In one story, two young hero- ines, highly sensitive in the accepted style, "faint alternately on a sofa." In another, an infant girl is discovered, perfectly un- harmed and already able to talk, under a haystack. In a third, a young man has "so dazzling a Beauty that none but Eagles could look him in the Face." People fall in love at the drop of a hat, children pilfer their parents' savings, and a man discovers four long-lost grandchildren in rapid succession.

In other words, Austen knew exactly what she was doing when she created her fiction of ordinary life. It didn't happen by default, as if she never really thought about it and simply did what came naturally. It was a revolutionary artistic choice, a courageous defiance of convention and expectation: exactly why so many of her early readers had trouble appreciating what she had done, and why her fame took so long to establish itself.

Yet she did more than reject the literary formulas of her day. Her own life may have seemed uneventful: she lived in a quiet corner of the English countryside, never married, never traveled more than about a hundred miles from home, didn't publish her first novel until she was thirty-five, and died, still sharing a house with her mother and sister, just six years later. But she lived amid a host of dramatic events, both global in scope and closer to home. Born in 1775, the year that launched the American Revolution, she was a teenager during the French Revolution and an adult during the Napoleonic Wars—a quarter century of epic struggle between Great Britain and France that climaxed at Waterloo just two years before her death. Her life also coincided with the most dynamic phase of the conquest of India, and thus, the rise of the British Empire.

Though they seem remote from her quiet existence, these events touched her very closely. Her father's bright, pretty sister, endowed with the striking name of Philadelphia, went out to India as a young woman, like so many girls at the time, to find herself a husband from among the mass of ambitious young men who had gone to the booming colony to seek their fortune. Not only did she find one, she may have also found a lover in the person of Warren Hastings, the brilliant young administrator who was on his way to becoming the first governor-general of India and one of the most important figures in the history of the Raj. From then on, the Austen and Hastings families would remain intertwined. Philadelphia, childless for the first eight years of her marriage, gave birth to a daughter within two years of meeting her husband's new business associate. The girl's name, Eliza, was the same as that of Hastings's daughter, who had died in infancy. Hastings, a widower, not only acted as Eliza's godfather and later gave her the spanking sum of ten thousand pounds, he also sent his young son back to England to be raised in the home of Philadelphia's newly married brother—that is, Jane Austen's father himself.

Austen never knew the boy, for he died of diphtheria within a few months. But she did come to know her cousin Eliza, who went on to live another remarkable story, very well indeed. Philadelphia had returned to England along with her husband when their daughter was three. When Eliza was nineteen—she had grown up to be a lively, beautiful, and flirtatious young woman—she married a French count and acquired the glamorous name of Capot de Feuillide. A few years later—Jane was ten by now—Madame de Feuillide descended upon the Austens' sleepy parsonage in all the glory of her French stories and French fashions. Despite the age difference, the two cousins formed a close and loving friendship that lasted to the end of the older woman's life.

Meanwhile, Warren Hastings, returned to England after

twelve years as the master of British India, was impeached for corruption by the House of Commons and embroiled in the most spectacular trial of Austen's day. The ordeal dragged on for seven years, followed by the Austens with intense partisanship on behalf of their patron, and finally ended in Hastings's acquittal. By that point, however, Eliza had become entangled in the French Revolution. Her husband lost his estates; Madame la Comtesse, as she liked to be called, was prevented from returning to France; and at last—Eliza herself was probably taking refuge with the Austens at the time—the count himself was sent to the guillotine. And then, before long, in a turn toward the family with which she had become so close, Eliza married Austen's older brother Henry, ten years younger than herself.

The Napoleonic Wars came even closer to home. Two of Austen's other brothers (she had six in all) joined the Royal Navy, Britain's proudest institution and first line of defense— Frank, a year older than she, and Charles, the baby, four years younger. Frank sailed to the Far East, fought in the Mediterranean, made captain by the age of twenty-six, narrowly missed the great victory at Trafalgar—a bitter regret—but chased the French across the Atlantic, played a leading role in the Battle of San Domingo, the last major naval engagement of the conflict, and fought the Americans in the War of 1812. Charles, less lucky in his career, still saw his share of perilous action, helping to run down one French warship in a chase of some two hundred miles, capturing another from a small boat in a heavy storm, hunting Napoleon's allies after the emperor's escape from Elba, and fighting Greek pirates in the Aegean. Austen, needless to say, followed all of these events—by letter, by rumor, through newspaper reports, and in her brothers' own stories when they returned home on leave—with breathless interest.

Her neighbors were scarcely less colorful. The cast of characters included "military heroes, bastard sprigs of the aristocracy, ruined squires," and "brilliant factory-owners of foreign origin," as Austen biographer Claire Tomalin enumerates them. One, Lord Portsmouth, was a feebleminded aristocrat with a macabre taste for funerals and slaughterhouses. After his first wife died, he was swindled into marrying his lawyer's daughter (Lord Byron was a witness, though he seemed unaware of what was going on), who proceeded to dismiss the servants and tyrannize her husband with regular whippings and beatings—gothic stuff indeed.

Tales of India and France, high-seas adventure and high-society scandal—godsends, it would seem, for any novelist in search of material. Yet Austen turned them all aside with a polite smile. Rather than Warren Hastings and Elizabeth Capot de Feuillide, she preferred to write about people like Mr. Woodhouse and Harriet Smith. Instead of Napoleonic battles and clandestine torture, she chose the dramatic possibilities of card parties and country picnics. She knew what she was about, and refused all temptations to wander from her course. After *Emma* was dedicated, at his own invitation, to the prince regent—Great Britain's acting monarch during the senility of his father, George III—Austen heard again from the prince's librarian, a pompous clergyman named James Stanier Clarke, who had been serving as the regent's intermediary. (The prince did not of course deal with Austen himself, even if she was one of his favorite writers.) Clarke took the liberty of inflicting upon her that common torment of successful authors: he gave her an idea for a book. "Any Historical Romance illustrative of the History of the august house of Cobourg," the German noble family whose youngest son was about to marry the Prince's daughter, "would just now be very interesting," he helpfully explained.

"I am fully sensible that an Historical Romance . . . might be much more to the purpose of Profit or Popularity, than such pictures of domestic Life in Country Villages as I deal in," Austen replied ("romance" here meaning something like "saga")—

> but . . . I could not sit seriously down to write a serious Romance under any other motive than to save my Life, & if it were indispensable for me to keep it up & never relax into laughing at myself or other people, I am sure I should be hung before I had finished the first Chapter.—No—I must keep to my own style & go on in my own Way.

Her own way was to make art out of the very things that absorbed her attention in her own life. No one was closer to her than her older sister, Cassandra, with whom she shared a room until the end of her life. The two exchanged hundreds of letters during their periods of separation, filled with exactly the kind of gossipy detail that Austen shaped so gloriously into her novels:

> Martha & I dined yesterday at Deane to meet the Powletts & Tom Chute. . . . Mrs. Powlett was at once expensively & na-

kedly dress'd;—we have had the satisfaction of estimating
her Lace and her Muslin [in other words, guessing how much
they cost]*; & she said too little to afford us much other*
amusement.—Mrs. John Lyford is so much pleased with the
state of widowhood as to be going to put in for being a
widow again;—she is to marry a Mr. Fendall, . . . a man of
very good fortune, but considerably older than herself.

You will not expect to hear that I was asked to dance—but
I was—by the Gentleman whom we met that Sunday with
Capt. D'auvergne. We have always kept up a Bowing ac-
quaintance since, & being pleased with his black eyes, I
spoke to him at the Ball, which brought on me this civility;
but I do not know his name,—& he seems so little at home
in the English Language that I beleive his black eyes may be
the best of him.

The Tables are come, & give general contentment. . . .
They are both covered with green baize & send their
best Love.—The Pembroke has got its destination by the
sideboard. . . .—The little Table which used to stand
there, has most conveniently taken itself off into the best
bed-room. . . .—So much for that subject; I now come to
another, of a very different nature, as other subjects are very
apt to be. . . .

And so on and so forth, for pages at a time of wit, silliness,
high spirits, family news, gowns, weather, dances, and colds.
Jane Austen's life may have *seemed* uneventful compared to her

aunt's or cousin's or brothers', or indeed, compared to just about anyone's. Her genius began with the recognition that such lives as hers were very eventful indeed—that every life is eventful, if only you know how to look at it. *She* did not think that her existence was quiet or trivial or boring; she thought it was delightful and enthralling, and she wanted us to see that our own are, too. She understood that what fills our days should fill our hearts, and what fills our hearts should fill our novels.

If I was so slow to catch on to all this, there was, of course, a very good reason. I'm a guy, after all. We aren't exactly taught to pay attention to "minute particulars." Gossip, we're told, is for women. The very word is feminine, derogatory, trivializing. Like Emma and Mrs. Weston, or Jane Austen and Cassandra, it is women who are supposed to spend half hours, and more than half hours, gabbing with their girlfriends about every little thing. We are expected to preserve a manly silence, or speak only of impersonal matters—in other words, girls, gear, and sports or, if we take ourselves very seriously, politics and public affairs.

Things were not any different in Austen's day, as the way she used that very phrase "minute particulars" made a point of underscoring. Mr. Knightley, a family friend, was telling the heroine some very interesting news about Harriet Smith. But when Emma pressed him for the juicy details, Knightley threw up his hands in masculine exasperation. "Your friend Harriet will make a much longer history when you see her," he said.

"She will give you all the minute particulars, which only woman's language can make interesting.—In our communications we deal only in the great."

The last word was a joke—Knightley was not that self-important—but other than that, he meant what he said. Women make "long histories," long stories, but men do not. Austen meant it, too, but she also meant, I realized as I read the scene, a lot more than Knightley could know. I was only about a dozen pages from the end of the novel, and she was using him, I saw, to expound her artistic theory and declare her artistic triumph. "Women's language"—the idiom of everyday conversation—was exactly the language in which *Emma* was written, and making those minute particulars interesting was precisely what Austen had done. She had given us a long history of private matters, of what Emma had called, many pages back, "woman's friendship and woman's feelings." She had gossiped with us for four hundred pages, made us her girlfriends, told us of "little affairs, arrangements, perplexities, and pleasures," and we had listened and understood, because she had been always interesting and always intelligible.

She had shown us, in other words, what it means to see and think and talk like a woman. The very idea that those things might be worth my while would have been ridiculous to me before I encountered her. Just the previous semester, in fact, I had loudly and proudly expressed the general male attitude toward "chick lit." It was in a seminar in popular fiction run by a famously macho professor—an aging Clark Gable look-alike, six foot three with a cigarette rasp, who told stories about hanging out in the Village back in the jazz days and getting

punched in the stomach by Norman Mailer. After weeks of
boyish fun—*Frankenstein* and *Dracula*, Sherlock Holmes and
Edgar Allan Poe, *I, the Jury* and *The Maltese Falcon*—we got
to Daphne du Maurier's *Rebecca* (the book that inspired the
Hitchcock movie), a chick-lit novel if there ever was one. As
soon as the session started, the professor sensed the torpor in
the room.

"What's the matter?" he asked the class of mostly guys.
"Didn't you like it?"

"I don't know," I said, always the first to volunteer my opinion. "I can't really relate to it. It's kind of—girlie."

The guys responded with a murmur of assent, while one of
the female students noted that although women learn to cross-
identify with male heroes—out of necessity, if nothing else,
since that's what literature mainly gives you—men are only ever
asked to identify with other men.

But there I was, just a few months later, soaking up the girli-
est novelist of all, the godmother of chick lit. Austen had shown
me what it meant to act like a woman, and she'd also made me
recognize why it was worthwhile. She had taught me to listen
to people like Mr. Woodhouse or Miss Bates, not just because
they deserved the same respect as everybody else, and not just
because their feelings were as real and as deep, but because I
might actually have important things to learn from them. Indeed, once I started paying attention to those two, it slowly
dawned on me that however silly they might be, they each possessed a vital piece of wisdom—each embodied, in fact, one of
the very lessons the novel itself was trying to teach.

Mr. Woodhouse may have been overbearing, with his obsessions about health and food—"Mrs. Bates, let me propose your venturing on one of these eggs. An egg boiled very soft is not unwholesome. Serle understands boiling an egg better than any body"—but they grew from a genuinely tender concern for the well-being of those around him. Here he was, "the kind-hearted, polite old man," talking to Jane Fairfax, Miss Bates's niece, "with all his mildest urbanity":

> *I am very sorry to hear, Miss Fairfax, of your being out this morning in the rain. . . . Young ladies are delicate plants. They should take care of their health and their complexion. . . . I hope your good grand-mama and aunt are well. They are some of my very old friends. I wish my health allowed me to be a better neighbour. You do us a great deal of honour to-day, I am sure. My daughter and I are both highly sensible of your goodness, and have the greatest satisfaction in seeing you at Hartfield.*

This was magnificently sweet, among the most touching moments in the book, and as an argument for simple human kindness—the concern for other people's feelings that Emma so conspicuously failed to show, and that I was so clueless about myself—impossible to disagree with.

As for Miss Bates, she lived the novel's highest lesson of all. Here was how Austen introduced her:

> *Her youth had passed without distinction, and her middle of life was devoted to the care of a failing mother, and the endeavour to make a small income go as far as possible. And*

yet she was a happy woman. . . . She loved every body, was
interested in every body's happiness, quicksighted to every
body's merits; thought herself a most fortunate creature, and
surrounded with blessings.

Emma, who had it all, was forever discontented with the world
around her—just like me, in my perpetual fog of resentful
gloom. Instead it was Miss Bates—scraping by, facing a lonely
old age, dependent on everybody else's goodwill—who was the
happy one. If her speech bubbled and flowed in an endless
stream of little matters, that was only because, like Austen herself, she found everything around her so very interesting.

To pay attention to "minute particulars" is to notice your life
as it passes, before it passes. But it is also, I realized, something
more. By talking over their little daily affairs—and not just
talking them over, but talking them over and over, again and
again (the same story in brief, then in full, the same stories in
one house, then another)—the characters in *Emma* were doing
nothing less than attaching themselves to life. They were weaving the web of community, one strand of conversation at a
time. They were creating the world, in the process of talking
about it.

Yet again, it was Emma herself who had trouble with this.
She loved to gossip with her special friend Mrs. Weston, of
course, but when Miss Bates started in, she couldn't get away
fast enough, and Jane Fairfax's letters were a fate worse than
death. She was the cleverest and best-looking person around,

and richer and more wellborn than just about everyone else, and she thought she deserved a more interesting life than the one that was on offer in Highbury. Like a bad reader, she was looking for intrigue and adventure, but all she ended up doing was cutting herself off from the people around her. And as a result, she cut herself off from herself. The fun of *Emma* was the way that the heroine, with her supreme confidence in her own judgment, was always screwing up, but the reason wasn't that much fun at all. Like me, she was numb. She couldn't feel what she felt, or know what she wanted.

But Emma finally learned that everyday life is not only more joyful—and more dramatic—than she could have imagined, it is also more joyful and more dramatic than anything she *did* imagine, any of her plots or daydreams. With those, she just played at feeling. But dull old, trivial old everyday life—that is where feeling truly lies. Finding that out, she found out whom she should marry, and I found out that this was where the novel had been heading all along. It really *had* had its heroine's romantic future on its mind, but its mind turned out to be very, very deep. In the end *Emma* didn't lack a plot; its plot was so clever that it could keep itself hidden until the very last, when all of its disparate parts leaped into order in a single instant, like iron filings around a magnet.

Emma's life finally became real to her, and in reading about her life I felt mine finally becoming real to me. Sleepwalking through my days just wasn't going to cut it anymore. Reading *Emma*, being asked to take the lives of characters like Harriet Smith and Jane Fairfax as seriously as they did themselves— not the exciting lives of heroes and heroines, which were so enjoyable to identify with, or the glamorous lives of celebrities, which were so much fun to read about, or the impressive lives of whatever big shots I happened to be remotely acquainted with, which made me feel so important, but the everyday lives of ordinary people, which matter for the sole reason that they *are* lives—made me finally begin to take my own life seriously.

Not that I hadn't always taken my plans and grand ambitions seriously—of course I had. What I hadn't taken seriously were the little events, the little moments of feeling, that my life actually consisted of. I wasn't Stephen Dedalus or Conrad's Marlow. I was Emma. I was Jane Fairfax. I was Miss Bates. I wasn't a rebel, I was a fool. I wasn't floating in splendid isolation a million miles above the herd. I was part of the herd. I was a regular person, after all. Which means, I was a person.

If I started to take my life seriously for the first time, I also started to take the world seriously. Again, I would have been surprised at the idea that I didn't already take it very seriously indeed. Hadn't I always worried about the big issues—politics, social justice, the future? Didn't I spend a lot of time arguing about them with my friends, deciding how everything should be? But ultimately, all that talk was just theoretical, no more real in the feelings it involved than Emma's ideas for rearranging the lives of the people around her. Austen taught me a new kind of moral seriousness—taught me what moral seriousness really means. It means taking responsibility for the little world, not the big one. It means taking responsibility for yourself.

As I read my way through *Emma,* my life began to acquire a sense of weight I had never experienced before. It was like one of those astounding moments when you look around at the world and really see it for the first time, feel its presence as a reality instead of just a bunch of concepts: water really *is* wet, the sky really *is* blue, this world really *is* the only one we have. As Virginia Woolf, Jane Austen's most perceptive reader, had the heroine in *Mrs. Dalloway* reflect, "it was very, very dangerous to live even one day." Not because life is so perilous, but because it is so momentous.

My ideas about literature were no more able to survive these revelations than were my ideas about anything else. Having worshipped at the altar of modernism, with its arrogant postures and lofty notions of philosophical significance, I believed that great literature had to be forbidding and esoteric: full of allusions that flaunted their own learning, dense with images and symbols that had to be pieced together like a giant jigsaw puzzle. A book, to be really valuable, had to offer truths that seemed as recondite as metaphysics and as final as Scripture— had to promise to reveal the nature of language, or the self, or time. Modernism was superior art for superior people, or so that snobbiest of literary movements believed. No wonder I disdained the herd; I'd learned that pose from T. S. Eliot and Vladimir Nabokov, every line of whose work strutted its contempt for ordinary people. *Emma* refuted the notion that great literature must be difficult, and it also rebuked the human attitudes that that idea was designed to justify. I still loved modernism, I just no longer believed it was the only way to make art, and I certainly didn't think that it was way to live.

Yet what of that modernist novel par excellence, the work

that formed the very core of my identity as a reader: James Joyce's *Ulysses*? As any English major can tell you, *Ulysses* also celebrates the everyday. With it, Joyce sought to create a work that was comparable in artistic majesty and cosmic scope to the great epics of Homer, Virgil, and Dante, the summit of Western literature, but at its center he placed, not a heroic figure like Achilles or Odysseus, but the most unremarkable man he could think of, a Jewish advertising agent named Leopold Bloom—a sad sack, a cuckold, a loner, a loser. The novel's epic grandeur comes instead from the symbolic structures that Joyce builds around him, starting with the title. Unbeknownst to the man himself, Bloom becomes a modern-day Ulysses, his single day's journey around Dublin a contemporary equivalent, in minia-ture, of his predecessor's ten years of wandering among gods and monsters.

The gesture is exhilarating, even ennobling. Like Austen, Joyce was saying that every life, including yours, is heroic in its own way. But the reason *Ulysses* had never brought me to the recognitions that *Emma* did was precisely the means by which Joyce had chosen to say it. So obtrusive were those symbolic structures, so ostentatious were Joyce's artistic effects, that you finally got the sense that Bloom's importance had nothing whatsoever to do with Bloom and everything to do with his creator. Bloom's robes were borrowed; it was not his life that was worthy of our notice after all, but the artistic treatment to which that life had been subjected. The figure Bloom's story ultimately magnifies is Joyce himself—the one incomparable artist, not the everyman. From this perspective, the message of *Ulysses* was the very opposite of Austen's. Ordinary life is important only because of what a James Joyce can do with it. Aside from that, your life isn't very important at all.

As it happens, someone once tried to tell me about a theory she had heard that *Emma* itself—by critical consensus Austen's greatest work—was designed to be a kind of epic, too, Austen's subtler contribution to the same high tradition that Joyce would so loudly seek to enter a century later. The picnic episode, where Emma hit bottom, morally speaking, was supposed to be the novel's version of the hero's descent to the underworld, the central convention of Western epic, and so on and so forth. This, keep in mind, was a fan of Austen who was making me this argument; to her, it exalted her favorite author to the status of the big boys. But to me, it utterly missed the point of what Austen was trying to do—even, in a sense, disparaged it. We don't need to pretend that Austen's novels are really epics in disguise in order to value them as highly as they deserve. She didn't need to play the same game as the big boys. Her small, feminine game was every bit as good, and every bit as grand. Austen glorified the everyday on its *own* terms—without the glamour of Joyce, and modernism, and epic archetypes, and the whole repertoire of epic conventions. What she offered us, if we're willing to see it, is *just* the everyday, without amplification. *Just* the novel, without excuses. Just the personal, just the private, just the little, without apologies.

There was one more thing about my life that had to change, now that I'd read *Emma*: my relationships with the people around me. Once I started to see myself for the first time, I started seeing *them* for the first time, too. I began to notice and care about what they might be experiencing, and they began to develop the depth and richness of literary characters. I could almost feel along with their feelings now, as we talked, feel the contours of them as they tried to express them to me. Instead of a boring blur, the life around me now was sharp and important. Everything was interesting, everything was meaningful, every conversation held potential revelations. It was like having my ears turned on for the first time. Suddenly the world seemed fuller and more spacious than I had ever imagined it could be, a house with a thousand rooms that now lay open to explore.

Above all, I started paying attention to what the people around me might be feeling and experiencing in relation to *me*— how the things I said and did affected them. Surprise, surprise, a lot of those things really pissed them off. If you're oblivious to other people, chances are pretty good that you're going to hurt them. I knew now that if I was ever going to have any real friends—or I should say, any real friendships with my friends— I'd have to do something about it. I'd have to somehow learn to stop being a defensive, reactive, self-enclosed jerk.

I was talking with one of those friends one day around this time. She was an old girlfriend from college, someone I knew I had not been very nice to back in the day, and she was telling me about one of her other friends, how she'd been feeling lately that they were no longer as intimate as they once had been. As I listened to her talk about a relationship that had clearly been far closer than any I had ever experienced, I started to get more and more agitated, until I finally had to break in. "Well," I demanded, "what does intimacy mean?" It wasn't a rhetorical question. I suddenly realized that it was terribly important, and that I didn't know. And then, with the most plaintive sense of bewilderment and loss—as if there were this giant thing out there that had been going on for years that I'd just discovered I was totally missing out on but had no clue how to find—I added, "Are *we* intimate? Is *this* intimacy, what we're having right now?" I really had no idea, but the look on her face said it all. "You poor bastard," it told me. "Of course we're not. Of course this isn't."

Well, it just sat there, that realization, like a lump in my gut—sat there for weeks. I didn't know what to do with it, how to get rid of it, how to dig myself out of the hole I'd just discovered I was in. But I knew that I couldn't live like that anymore. By the end of the school year, I gathered up the courage to talk to my girlfriend and tell her that we had to break up. Even if I was beginning to understand what a real relationship should look like, we still didn't have very much in common, and besides, I had botched this one so badly there was no way to start over. (In fact, she had figured out that we needed to break up a long time before I did and was just as relieved to be done with it.) Being alone wasn't going to be easy after such a long time, but I knew that if I was ever going to get anywhere as a human being, that would have to be the first step. Or no, that wasn't the first step. The first step had been reading *Emma*.

CHAPTER 2

pride and prejudice
growing up

Those first years in graduate school, I lived in a dingy little university apartment that I shared with a random series of business students who'd been assigned to the same space. They would go to corporate-sponsored happy hours and come back flushed with cocktails and job prospects, or bring their friends back to the apartment and whoop it up in front of the TV. I'd hole up in my room, burrowing like a hamster. And quite a little den it was. My desk was a slab of wood over two filing cabinets; my bed was a pancaked old futon that I rolled right out on the floor. A hard chair, a narrow bookcase, a secondhand computer—that was pretty much it. I would sleep till noon, then stay up reading until four or five in the morning, blocking the glare from the security lights in the airshaft with an old woolen blanket that hung from a couple of nails I had pounded into the window frame. When it was time for my 3:00 A.M. dinner of ramen noodles or English-muffin pizza, I'd wait a few seconds after turning on the kitchen light, to give the roaches a chance to hide.

I was in my late twenties, in other words, and still living like a college student. I was having trouble growing up—one of the reasons, in fact, that I'd gone back to school in the first place. I'd been out in the world for a few years, had had a couple of jobs, but I still hadn't learned how to cope with life on my own. Simple things, like buying a bottle of shampoo, would make me catatonic with confusion. I'd stand there in the store with the bottle in my hand like a sleepwalker who had just woken up, wondering how I had gotten there and what I was supposed to do next. *Yes, right,* I would think. *You've come in here because you need this. To wash your hair. Now go to the front of the store and pay for it.*

If I was having trouble becoming an adult, it wasn't a big surprise. As the youngest in a family of three kids—and the youngest by a lot, almost six years—I had always been treated like the baby. My mother was very loving and supportive—I was "her" child, the one who looked like her and reminded her of her own adored father—yet she also tended to infantilize me. But the more important presence was my father, the figure who dominated the household. Simultaneously demanding and undermining, he infantilized me *without* being loving and supportive. He expected everything, but he gave me the unmistakable message that he didn't really think I could do anything.

In retrospect, it's clear that he was haunted by a sense of

financial and even physical insecurity. He and his parents had been refugees from World War II, having escaped from Europe—that is, from the Holocaust—at the last possible moment. Much of his family had not escaped, and although he had erased his Czech accent by sheer force of will, he was still profoundly marked by his early experiences. He never spent a dime he didn't have to, never threw away so much as a paper clip. With us he was not only stern and withholding, a shouter and hitter who demanded top grades, he was also overprotective to the point of being overbearing.

He didn't want his sons to take risks or explore options or strike out on our own; he wanted us to follow the plan that he'd laid out for us: major in science—he was an engineer himself—go to medical school, and start earning a living as quickly as possible. Don't waste time, don't get distracted. The world was a dangerous place, and the fewer wrong turns you made, the better. He'd figured out what you needed to do to ensure yourself a secure life, and there was no point in our figuring it out all over again for ourselves.

When my father saw me struggling with something—whether I was ten and having trouble opening a jar or fifteen and trying to write a paper—he would rush in and take care of it instead of letting me work things out on my own. His intentions were good; he wanted to save me the pain and trouble of floundering around until I got it right. "I've already made those mistakes," he would say. "I want you to learn from my experience." But his strategy overlooked the fact that he wasn't always going to be there to take care of me. So I never learned how to look after myself, how to deal with salespeople or handle money, how to make my own way in the world. There I was, twenty-eight years old and still staring at the shampoo.

I hadn't helped myself by going back to school at Columbia. My father was on the faculty, and because it had been free for us, I had already gone there for college. I could have gone to Chicago this time, but the prospect of moving to an unfamiliar city, hundreds of miles away from almost anyone I knew, was not something I could even begin to imagine. So there I was again, back in the same old place, living in an apartment that was practically around the corner from his office.

I'd drop by every once in a while, and he would take me out for Chinese food. He wasn't very happy that I was studying English—he figured he would wind up supporting me for the rest of his life—and we would struggle about it over the chow fun. "If I had my own business," he would say, "I would offer to take you in. But you wouldn't do it anyway!" I'd remind him that that was exactly what had happened between him and his own father, who had owned a little business in the Garment District (my father hadn't wanted to sell zippers any more than I wanted be a doctor), but it didn't cut much ice.

The fact is, he never thought I'd get through graduate school. He hadn't even thought I'd get *in* to graduate school. Whatever the next challenge was, he was sure I couldn't meet it. After all—the logic was perfectly circular—hadn't he always had to help me out with everything? He didn't think I'd make the cut after the first year, and because I'd gotten C's in high-school French—he spoke six languages himself—he was sure I'd never complete my language requirements. "I appreciate the support," I'd say, and then I'd thank him for lunch and head back to my crummy apartment.

I was living in that apartment when I read *Emma* and broke it off with my girlfriend, and I was still living there a year later when I read my way through the rest of Jane Austen. It was the summer after my third year in graduate school. I had finished my courses (and yes, completed my language requirements), and now I was studying for the dreaded oral qualifying exams, which I would have to take that fall. It was the ultimate academic endurance test. I had four months to read about a hundred books, and then I'd be shut in a room with four professors who would grill me about them for two hours. It was also a rite of passage. Once I got through it—*if* I got through it—I'd be one step closer, in professional terms, to growing up and becoming one of those professors myself. (My father, of course, was sure I'd never pass. "You have your work cut out for you!" he said.) As for growing up in any other sense, I still didn't see that I might have a problem.

I had the place to myself that summer—the second of the business students, a rich preppy from Dartmouth, had cleared out for nicer digs—and I read from the time I got up until the time I went to sleep. I read while I was brushing my teeth, I read while I was eating my ramen noodles, I even read while I was walking down the street (which takes a fair amount of coordination, I discovered). And one of those days, about halfway through the summer, I very suddenly, and very unexpectedly, fell in love.

The object of my infatuation, of course, was Elizabeth Bennet. Why should I have been able to resist the heroine of *Pride and Prejudice* any better than anyone else? She was the most charming character I had ever met. Brilliant, witty, full of fun and laughter—the kind of person who makes you feel more alive just by being around. When her older sister, Jane, was gushing that a certain new acquaintance was "just what a young man ought to be," "sensible, good-humoured, lively," Elizabeth dryly replied, "He is also handsome, which a young man ought likewise to be, if he possibly can." Yet Elizabeth was also strong and openhearted and brave, the devoted friend who'd protect you like a lioness. When Jane got sick while visiting some wellborn friends at a nearby estate, Elizabeth thought nothing of tramping three miles through the mud to take care of her—and didn't give a damn if her sister's friends thought it made her look déclassé to do so.

Like me, Elizabeth had a difficult family to deal with. Jane was a dream—sweet, kind, patient, the perfect confidante. But their three little sisters were impossible. Mary, the middle girl, was a pedantic bore who got all her ideas from books ("Vanity and pride are different things, though the words are often used synonymously . . ."). Kitty and Lydia, the youngest two, were empty-headed flirts. Their father was a clever man—I sat up a little straighter every time he opened his mouth, and his relationship with Elizabeth was fun and playful—but he spent most of his energy sparring with their ridiculous mother, an overwrought bundle of foolishness. The two of them were like a long-running comedy act, and all the worse because they knew it. "You take delight in vexing me," Mrs. Bennet complained. "You have no compassion on my poor nerves." "You mistake me, my dear," her husband shot back. "I have a high respect for your nerves. They are my old friends. I have heard you mention them with consideration these last twenty years at least."

I also loved the fact that Elizabeth had as little interest in getting married as I did (and with parents like hers, who could blame her?). "If I were determined to get a rich husband," she remarked at one point, "or any husband . . ." Of course, that didn't stop her mother from having her own ideas. As the curtain opened, Mrs. Bennet, whose every waking thought was devoted to getting her daughters married, was nagging her husband to introduce himself to Charles Bingley, a wealthy young man who had just moved in to the neighborhood, before the other mothers could get their hands on him.

Soon the sisters had met both him and his even wealthier friend, Mr. Darcy. The two couldn't have been more different. Bingley was as cheerful and eager as a beagle. "Upon my honour," he told his friend at the first ball, "I never met with so many pleasant girls in my life as I have this evening." But Darcy was as haughty as a Siamese cat, practically licking himself clean whenever someone touched him the wrong way. He even had the gall to snub Elizabeth before he had so much as met her. "She is tolerable," Darcy protested when his friend suggested that he ask her to dance, "but not handsome enough to tempt *me*"—a statement I took as a personal affront. What kind of idiot would not find Elizabeth Bennet every bit as adorable as I did? The heroine agreed. While her sister and Bingley fell quickly in love (he was the "just what a young man ought to be" whom Jane was gushing about), she wrote Darcy down as an insufferable prig. Soon a third young man arrived who, having known Darcy as a child, confirmed all of her suspicions about his character.

Darcy, meanwhile, viewed Bingley's courtship with alarm, and he was not one to keep his opinions to himself. Not only was Jane beneath his friend in social terms, but other than herself and Elizabeth, their entire family was unspeakably vulgar. A dance at Bingley's sealed Jane's fate. Everyone was there, providing the Bennets with the maximum opportunity to make a spectacle of themselves. Mrs. Bennet crowed loudly about the impending match—"It was, moreover, such a promising thing for her younger daughters, as Jane's marrying so greatly must throw them in the way of other rich men"—oblivious to the way she was coming across and the fact that the wrong people might be listening. "What is Mr. Darcy to me," she snorted, when Elizabeth tried to quiet her down, "that I should be afraid of him?" Mary, with more affectation than talent, tried to show off, badly, on the piano. And as for the Bennets' clergyman cousin, Mr. Collins, one of the greatest fools in literary history, pompous and obsequious at the same time ("I consider the clerical office as equal in point of dignity with the highest rank in the kingdom—provided that a proper humility of behaviour is at the same time maintained"), he committed the unpardonable faux pas of addressing himself to Mr. Darcy without a formal introduction.

Elizabeth cringed at every turn—if "her family made an agreement to expose themselves as much as they could during the evening, it would have been impossible for them to play their parts with more spirit or finer success"—and I suffered along with her. Her family was blowing it for Jane, the only one of them, other than Elizabeth herself, who was worth a damn. But it was too late; Darcy had seen enough. He didn't care, it seemed, that his friend and Jane were in love. The next thing the Bennets knew, the young men were gone, and it looked like they'd never see Bingley again. Jane was crushed. Elizabeth was furious. I wanted to wring Darcy's neck.

This was a completely different experience than reading *Emma,* and not just because I'd already become a convert. *Emma* showed me from the very beginning just how desperately wrong its heroine was. I couldn't stand her—until Austen showed me how much I resembled her. But here I was, halfway through *Pride and Prejudice,* and not only was I head over heels for Elizabeth, I agreed with everything she said and every judgment she made. I loved her friends and hated her enemies. I would have taken her side against the world.

But then, as if a switch had been flipped, everything got turned upside down. Elizabeth ran into someone she never expected to see again. He made a declaration she never expected to hear. She lashed out in a fit of resentment. He responded with a long, coolly argued letter that threw all the events of the first half of the novel into a completely different light. She read it once and rejected its claims. She read it again—and suddenly saw she'd been utterly wrong all along.

Because Jane's love for Bingley was so clear to her, Elizabeth now realized, she'd assumed that it was clear to everyone else. Because her sister was so wonderful, she'd refused to believe, when push came to shove, that their family's behavior would prevent Jane from marrying well. Because Elizabeth was so proud herself, she'd disdained the pride of others when she found it aimed in her direction. But worst of all, she now saw, was her judgment of character—the very thing on which she most congratulated herself. She had thought that she could read a man the very first time she met him. She had made the mistake of believing that if a young man was affable and friendly, he must be good, and that if he was cold and arrogant and reserved, he must be bad.

But now she saw how completely mistaken she'd been. Her verdict, delivered with all her characteristic bluntness and courage, was uncompromising: "blind, partial, prejudiced, absurd." "How despicably I have acted!" she exclaimed to herself. "I, who have prided myself on my discernment! I, who have valued myself on my abilities!"

But of course, if Elizabeth had been wrong about everything, then so had I. I had made the very same judgments that she had, and I had made them every bit as badly. This was indeed a different experience from reading *Emma*. That novel had invited me to laugh at its heroine, with all her ridiculous schemes. But this time, the joke was on me.

So enthralled had I been by Elizabeth's intelligence and charm that I had never once thought to question her. No doubt self-flattery had played a big role there. Austen had seduced me into identifying with her heroine, and I had been only too happy to comply. Now it turned out that if I did indeed re-semble her, it was not for the reasons I'd supposed. Elizabeth trusted her judgment way too much—just as I did. She was so much cleverer than everyone she knew except her father—who was always telling her how clever she was—that she imagined that everything she believed must be true, just because she be-lieved it. She didn't think she needed to give other people a fair hearing. What could they possibly have to say? She already knew everything she needed to know.

The novel's original title had been *First Impressions*. Eliza-beth was not prejudiced in the modern sense of the word. She didn't judge people before she met them, because of the group they belonged to. She judged them the moment she met them, because she thought she could already tell everything about them. "First impressions": it seemed to me now that the phrase did double duty. It referred to the heroine's tendency to jump to conclusions, and it also pointed to ours, as we put ourselves in her place.

There was a third meaning, too. "First" as in "early"—as in, the things that happen to you when you're first starting out in life. The novel, I saw, wasn't finally about prejudice, or pride, or even love. Elizabeth was all of twenty, and her mistakes were errors of youth—the mistakes, precisely, of a person who has never made mistakes, or at least, who has never been forced to acknowledge them. Beneath the polished wit that she flashed at the world like a suit of armor, Elizabeth was still scarcely more than a girl. "If I were determined to get a rich husband, or any husband": that was the statement, not of someone who knew what she wanted from life, but of someone who hadn't even started to figure it out. When she had her epiphany—"blind, partial, prejudiced, absurd"—she added a final count to her indictment: "Till this moment I never knew myself." Darcy's pride and Elizabeth's prejudice, his prejudice and her pride: these may have set the plot in motion, but by putting me through Elizabeth's experiences—by having her make mistakes and learn from them, and having me stumble and learn right there along with her—what the novel was really showing me was how to grow up.

Growing up may be the most remarkable thing that anybody ever does. One day we're hitting our little brother over the head with a wooden duck, and a few days later we're running a business, or writing a book, or raising a child of our own. How do we do it? The physical part is easy. A little food, a little exercise, and without ever having to think about it, we gradually find ourselves getting older, and taller, and hairier. But the other part—what about that? We come into the world as a tiny bundle of impulse and ignorance—how do we ever become fit for human company, let alone capable of love?

This, I discovered that summer, was what Jane Austen's novels were about. Her heroines were sixteen or nineteen or twenty (people married young in those days, especially women). We followed them for a few weeks, or a few months, or a year. They started out in one place, and gradually—or sometimes, quite suddenly—they ended up somewhere else. They opened their eyes, let out a scream, took a few frantic breaths, then settled down and looked around at the strange new world in which they'd come to find themselves. They started out as girls, and day by day, page by page, before our very eyes, they turned into women.

It was the way they did it, though, that came as such a revelation to me. I was used to thinking about growing up in terms of going to school and getting a job: passing tests, gaining admissions, accumulating credentials, acquiring the kinds of knowledge and skills that made you employable—the terms in which my parents (and everyone else, for that matter) had taught me to think about it. If I had been asked to consider what kinds of personal qualities it might involve—which I doubt I ever was—I would have spoken of things like self-confidence and self-esteem. As for anything like character or conduct, who even used such words anymore? Their very sound was harsh to me: so demanding, so inflexible. They made me think of school uniforms, and nuns with rulers, and cold baths on winter mornings—all the terrible things that people used to inflict on their children.

But Austen, it turned out, did not see things that way. For her, growing up has nothing to do with knowledge or skills, because it has everything to do with character and conduct. And you don't strengthen your character or improve your conduct by memorizing the names of Roman emperors (or American presidents) or learning how to do needlework (or calculus). You don't do so, she believed, by developing self-confidence and self-esteem, either. If anything, self-confidence and self-esteem are the great enemies, because they make you forget that you're still just a bundle of impulse and ignorance. For Austen, growing up means making mistakes.

That was the first lesson that *Pride and Prejudice* taught me. Elizabeth's errors were not accidents she could have avoided; they were expressions of her character—in fact, of the very best parts of her character, that quickness and confidence for which I loved her so. You don't "fix" your mistakes, Austen was telling me, as if they somehow existed outside you, and you can't prevent them from happening, either. You aren't born perfect and only need to develop the self-confidence and self-esteem with which to express your wondrous perfection. You are born with a whole novel's worth of errors ahead of you. No, my father couldn't save me from my mistakes, but maybe my mistakes could save me, from myself.

Elizabeth and I were young, and like most young people, we didn't see how young we really were. If anything, people in their twenties have the opposite idea about themselves. When he was Elizabeth's age, T. S. Eliot wrote poems about how terribly, terribly old he felt. It's that sense, now that your childhood is over, of being ever so jaded and world-weary and wise. You put on a trench coat or dress in black, to show how over it you are. You say "Whatever" a lot, or "Duh!"—because it's all just so boring and predictable. If you're Elizabeth Bennet, you swear you'll never marry, or you declare, about your very biggest mistake, "I beg your pardon;—one knows exactly what to think."

The amazing thing is just how serene Austen was about this. When most people think back to the way they behaved when they were young, they want to curl up in a ball, and when they see someone acting the same way now, they want to smack them in the head. But Austen observed it all with perfect humor and understanding. She sympathized with it, even though she recognized how foolish it was. But here's the really incredible thing. When she started working on *Pride and Prejudice*, she was still only twenty herself.

In writing about Elizabeth's situation, in other words, she was also writing about her own. Elizabeth loved to dance, and so did her author. Elizabeth loved to read, and so did her creator. Elizabeth loved to walk, and so did Jane Austen. As Elizabeth had Jane, so did Austen have Cassandra, a milder and properer two-years-older sister—confidante, sounding board, best friend—to adore and admire. ("If Cassandra were going to have her head cut off," their mother once said, "Jane would insist on sharing her fate.") Most importantly, Austen gave Elizabeth her own qualities of mind: a piercing wit and a wicked sense of humor. Like Elizabeth's high-wire conversations with Mr. Darcy, Austen's letters to Cassandra were an opportunity to show off both. Elizabeth said things like, "I am perfectly convinced . . . that Mr. Darcy has no defect. He owns it himself without disguise." Austen let herself go at greater length. Here she was, dishing the dirt on a ball she'd just attended:

There were very few Beauties, & such as there were, were not very handsome. Miss Iremonger did not look well, & Mrs. Blount was the only one much admired. She appeared ex-

actly as she did in September, with the same broad face, dia-
mond bandeau, white shoes, pink husband, & fat neck.—The
two Miss Coxes were there; I traced in one the remains of
the vulgar, broad featured girl who danced at Enham eight
years ago. . . .—I looked at Sir Thomas Champneys &
thought of poor Rosalie [a maid who'd caught his eye some
years before]; *I looked at his daughter & thought her a queer*
animal with a white neck.—Mrs. Warren, I was constrained
to think a very fine young woman, which I much regret. She
has got rid of some part of her child, & danced away with
great activity, looking by no means very large. Her husband
is ugly enough; uglier even than his cousin John; but he does
not look so very old.—The Miss Maitlands are both pretty-
ish; very like Anne; with brown skins, large dark eyes, & a
good deal of nose.—The General has got the Gout, & Mrs.
Maitland the Jaundice.—Miss Debary, Susan & Sally, all in
black, . . . made their appearance, & I was as civil to them
as their bad breath would allow me.

Ouch. But however wickedly she may have laughed at her neighbors in private, Austen went out of her way to protect their
feelings when it came to her public behavior. In the very same
letter—in fact, the very next thought—she talks of visiting a
friend the following Thursday, unless she stays for another ball
that night. But, she adds, "If I do not stay for the Ball, I would
not on any account do so uncivil a thing by the Neighborhood
as to set off at that very time for another place, & shall therefore make a point of not being later than Thursday *morning*."

Her sense of humor could be savage, but her heart was generous, and she endowed Elizabeth with that very same balance of wit and warmth. No wonder the heroine of *Pride and Prejudice* remained her author's favorite for the rest of her life. "I want to tell you that I have got my own darling Child from London," she wrote Cassandra upon receiving the first copies of the novel, and it's not entirely clear if she meant the book or its heroine. "I must confess," she went on, "that I think her as delightful a creature as ever appeared in print, & how I shall be able to tolerate those who do not like her at least, I do not know."

A few months later, on a trip to London, she searched the galleries for pictures of Elizabeth and Jane. "I was very well pleased," she wrote Cassandra, having found a painting that matched her mental image of the latter. "I went in hopes of seeing one of her Sister," she went on, but there was none to be found. "I can only imagine," she concluded, that Elizabeth's new husband "prizes any Picture of her too much to like it should be exposed to the public eye.—I can imagine he would have that sort of feeling—that mixture of Love, Pride & Delicacy." It's a lovely conceit, and it tells us two things. Austen was every bit as enraptured by Elizabeth's marriage as the heroine was herself, and no painting could measure up to Austen's image of her. The first person to fall in love with Elizabeth Bennet, it seems, was her creator.

All the more telling, then, that Austen didn't fool herself into thinking that her offspring was perfect. She knew that Elizabeth had a lot of growing up to do—which means that she recognized that she herself did, too. Indeed, as Austen grew older, her letters lost most of their sharpness and snark. Though she began *Pride and Prejudice* when she was barely out of her teens, it wasn't published until she was thirty-seven—*First Impressions*, the original version, was rejected by a publisher sight unseen, and she didn't return to it for many years—and by that point her letters made a very different sound than that free-swinging tale of the ball.

"Wisdom is better than Wit," she told her favorite niece around this time, "& in the long run will certainly have the laugh on her side." The niece, Fanny Knight, now twenty-one herself, was trying to decide whether to marry a certain young man, serious and thoughtful but a little wanting in manner and grace. Aunt Jane wasn't sure: did Fanny love him enough? But one thing she was certain of. "His uncommonly amiable mind, strict principles, just notions, good habits—*all* that *you* know so well how to value, *All* that really is of the first importance—everything of this nature pleads his cause most strongly." Good character, she was reminding her niece, is more important than liveliness and spirit.

Saying as much, she was watching over Fanny's own character, just as she had long done with all her brothers' many children (of whom she would live to see more than two dozen born). She wasn't a mother herself, but she had a mother's care for her nieces and nephews—especially Fanny and her siblings, her brother Edward's children, whose own mother died giving birth to the last. "They behave extremely well in every respect," she wrote of his two oldest boys, sent from boarding school to be cared for by their aunt and grandmother in the wake of the tragic event, "showing quite as much feeling as one wishes to see, and on every occasion speaking of their father with the liveliest affection."

Of her brother Charles's oldest girl, some years later, she was less complimentary: "That puss Cassy, did not shew more pleasure in seeing me than her Sisters, but I expected no better;—she does not shine in the tender feelings." "Nature has done enough for her—but Method" (i.e., what her parents have done) "has been wanting." Yet two years later, much of it spent under the guidance of Jane and Cassandra and their mother, little Cassy gave signs of improvement. "Her sensibility seems to be opening to the perception of great actions," her aunt wrote, and she has become, for her father, "a comfort." Soon, Austen was looking out for a new generation, her niece Anna's children. "Jemima has a very irritable bad Temper," she told a correspondent. "I hope as Anna is so early sensible of its' defects, that she will give Jemima's disposition the early & steady attention it must require."

The emphasis, as it always was when Austen wrote about children, was on character. Not beauty or creativity or even intelligence, but conduct and temperament and the capacity for empathy and feeling. She watched her nieces and nephews grow; she shaped that growth when she could; she knew that it would be a difficult process. Austen understood that kids are going to make mistakes, and she also understood that making mistakes is not the end of the world.

Finally, by reading *Pride and Prejudice*, I had come to understand it, too. Being right, Austen taught me, might get you a pat on the head, but being wrong could bring you something more valuable. It could help you find out who you are. Still, that wasn't the whole story. If I only needed to make mistakes, growing up would have been easy. I made mistakes all the time. In fact, I tended to make the same mistakes over and over again, just like Elizabeth. Making mistakes, I learned, was only the first step. Elizabeth's youngest sister, Lydia, loud, wild, and brazen, made flagrant mistakes all the time, too—yawning in people's faces, wasting money on trifles, shamelessly flirting with the young officers—and she was clearly never going to grow up. Elizabeth's mother's entire life was one long series of embarrassments, blunders, and miscalculations, including the whole way she raised her daughters and went about finding them husbands, yet she remained the same anxious, foolish, self-centered person that she'd always been.

It wasn't even enough, Austen showed me, to have your mistakes pointed out to you. Our brains are very good at figuring out what to say when people call us out on something that we've done. We scurry around like beavers, shoring up the walls of our self-esteem. Who, me? No, *you* must be wrong. That's not what I meant. Was it really such a big deal? It was an accident. It'll never happen again. That was the first time, I swear. Mistake? What mistake?

Austen's heroines, I discovered that summer, had their mistakes pointed out to them over and over again, only it never did them any good. They didn't grow up until something terrible finally happened. When maturity came to them, it came through suffering: through loss, through pain, above all, through humiliation. They did something really awful—not just stupid, but unjust and hurtful—and they did it right out in the open, in front of the very person whose opinion they cared about more than anyone else's. Emma insulted Miss Bates in the most callous fashion. Elizabeth leveled a whole series of mistaken accusations. And then someone forced them to see, in a way that they could not deny, just how very badly they had acted.

These were not easy scenes to read. They were almost as painful for me as they were for the heroines themselves. I grieved for these young women, because they were, at the moment of their humiliation, so very, very exposed. At first, all that most of them could do was burst into tears. Elizabeth was luckier. She learned the truth by letter, so at least she could be alone with her feelings. But the revelation of her many errors, when she finally did let it in, was no less crushing. She had been wrong about Jane, she had been wrong about her family, she had been wrong about everything. "Blind, partial, prejudiced, absurd": that wasn't just an intellectual judgment; it was a feeling that burned to the core. "How humiliating is this discovery!" she exclaimed to herself, "Yet, how just a humiliation!" And it was then, and only then, that she made her climactic discovery: "Till this moment I never knew myself."

In drama, this is known as the moment of recognition. Oedipus discovers his horrible crime. King Lear understands how terribly he has wronged his youngest daughter. Fortunately, the errors that Elizabeth made were neither so dire nor so final. *Pride and Prejudice* was a comedy, after all, not a tragedy, as stories about young people, who have time to correct their mistakes, usually are. But at that moment, after she had come to her awful knowledge, a tragedy was exactly what it looked as if the novel might become. Elizabeth not only saw how badly she had acted, she realized what it had cost her. A great happiness had been within her grasp, she now understood, and pride and prejudice had made her fling it away.

None of us, I knew, would ever wish this on ourselves, let alone on our children. But if we are lucky, Austen was telling me, it will happen nonetheless. Because my father was wrong: you can't learn from other people's mistakes; you can only learn from your own. Austen was making her beloved Elizabeth miserable because she knew that that's what growing up requires. For it is never enough to know that you have done wrong: you also have to feel it.

If there was ever a time that I felt it, it was that very summer. The truth is that Elizabeth Bennet was not the only woman I was in love with then. I was also in the throes of a gigantic crush on a woman I had met that spring. I was twenty-eight, she was twenty-one—the ages, come to think of it, of a hero and heroine in a Jane Austen novel. She was just graduating from college, and my feelings for her were an agonized confusion of desire and protectiveness. She was lovely and gentle and smart, with a slow smile that seemed to light up from within and an ironic sense of humor that came out with a raucous laugh. Our friendship flared up fast and bright. Here was someone, I saw, who could be a true companion.

My life got very simple that summer. My exams and her were the only things in it. Sharpening my brain against those hundred books, and wringing my heart for the want of her. The two ran together. She became my muse, my goal, the face that I saw when I looked through the page. Spending time in her company was the one exception I made to my rule of monastic seclusion. We would walk around the city, talking for hours about art and ideas and all the people we knew. We went to museums, we went to the theater, we would joke and compare notes and trade observations.

But none of it was any good. Because reliably, pretty much every time we got together, I would manage to say something idiotic and hurtful: pretentious or sexist or condescending. "Notice the way Matisse plays with color" (as if I were some kind of audio guide), or, "You should really read some more Freud" (though she'd probably read more than I had), or, "You'll understand these things when you get to be my age" (my age! all of twenty-eight!). It was a kind of compulsion. Reading *Emma* had helped me to become more aware of the people around me and how I affected them, and it certainly enabled me to become less callous and mean, and yet still, like Elizabeth, I thought I was just so damn smart that I couldn't stop myself from giving the rest of the world the benefit of my wisdom. My ego was so wrapped up in feeling superior that I had to parade it even (or maybe especially) to the person I loved. And every time I did, she would just look at me, wary but brave, and let me know what a complete jerk I was being. And every single time, I wanted to sink into the ground. Because I had blown it again; now, I thought, she would never want to be with me.

And in fact, she never did. She was my friend, but she never became my girlfriend. Yet the shame of it all, and the grief at what it had cost me, burned those lessons into my brain. She wasn't the first person to tell me I was arrogant and condescending—far, far from it—but because she mattered so much more to me than anyone ever had, she was the first to get through.

So when, after a couple of months of this, I read *Pride and Prejudice,* Elizabeth's experiences made perfect sense to me— or I should say made perfect sense *of* me, of what I had been going through. Our egos, Austen was telling me, prevent us from owning up to our errors and flaws, and so our egos must be broken down—exactly what humiliation does, and why it makes us feel so worthless. "Humiliation," after all, comes from "humility." It humbles us, makes us properly humble. So just as *Pride and Prejudice* taught me that it's okay to make mistakes, it also told me that it's okay to feel bad about them. Austen understood that growing up hurts—that it has to hurt, because otherwise it won't happen. And if it was too late, by the time I read the novel, to have the kind of happy ending that Elizabeth eventually did, it made me see that growing up can be a kind of happy ending in itself. Or at least, the promise of one to come.

Shame, humiliation, disgrace: hard feelings to accept if you've been brought up to believe that you should never have to experience any pain. In fact, Austen provided a perfect example of the kind of young person who doesn't accept them—Lydia

Bennet, Elizabeth's youngest sister—and what can happen as a result. Because Lydia was exactly like her mother—it was all too easy to imagine the empty-headed flirt that Mrs. Bennet must once have been—she had always been overindulged: never criticized, never restrained, coddled and fussed over no matter what she did. It was a classic case of overidentification: the mother eager to hold on to the last remnants of her youth by reliving it through her youngest daughter, the daughter only too happy to comply.

By the time she turned fifteen, Lydia was completely unmanageable. Always loud, always laughing, always flirting, never taking anything seriously—never taking her own life seriously. She was an embarrassment, and when she finally did something truly disgraceful, she became more than an embarrassment; she became a scandal. Yet there she was at the end of the novel, still laughing, still perfectly pleased with herself. "I am sure my sisters must all envy me," she somehow managed to say, though her sisters probably wanted to drown her in a lake. "I only hope they may have half my good luck." No matter how much pain she caused her family, Lydia was never going to feel the slightest bit of discomfort herself.

No suffering, no growth—and no recollection, no suffering. We have to see what we've done, we have to feel it, and finally, we have to remember it. Even after her disgrace, Lydia seemed to have "the happiest memories in the world. Nothing of the past was recollected with pain." Why was she able to have so clear a conscience about the things she'd done? Because she just pretended that they never happened. Nor was she the only one; the Bennets' whole social circle was no better. After they discovered the awful truth about a young gentleman with whom they had all been delighted, "every body declared that he was the wickedest young man in the world; and every body began to find out, that they had always distrusted the appearance of his goodness." It takes courage, Austen was telling us, to admit your mistakes, and even more courage to remember them.

How tempting it is to rewrite our personal history in a more flattering way, and how familiar we all are with the person who experiences a moment of self-knowledge—after a breakup or a failure or a sin—only to go right back to being the same person they always were. For Austen, maturation means refusing to forget. Humiliation, for her, is a gift that keeps on giving. "Think only of the past as its remembrance gives you pleasure," Elizabeth remarked at the end of the novel, but as usual, she was being ironic. In fact, she said it to the very person who she knew would keep her honest by continuing to point out her mistakes and remind her of what she had done.

Elizabeth had come to understand, at last, what growing up means, and she had also come to recognize that if you do it right, it never stops. Not only wasn't I born perfect, in other words, I was never going to be perfect, either. Becoming an adult was not going to give me the right to become complacent. Again, Austen offered a perfect example of what not to do. Elizabeth's father was a good man who had allowed his character to go to seed by choosing a wife who was never going to be able to challenge him, someone to whom it was far too easy to feel superior. Living with a woman like Mrs. Bennet had made him self-satisfied and morally lazy, and his children suffered as a result. He could have done a lot more to make his daughters financially secure, and when the great crisis came for his family, he turned out to be pretty much useless. If I was going to keep growing, Austen was telling me, I needed to stay on my toes. Fortunately, I had something to help me do so that Elizabeth and her father didn't. I had *Pride and Prejudice*.

Jane Austen was about a year old when another English author wrote a statement that could serve as a motto for all her books. "Life is a comedy for those who think," said Horace Walpole, "and a tragedy for those who feel." Everyone thinks, and everyone feels, but Jane Austen's question was, which are you going to put first? Comedies are stories with happy endings. I could grow up and find happiness, Austen was letting me know, but only if I was willing to give up something very important. Not my feelings, but my belief in my feelings, my conviction that they were always right.

This was not easy to swallow. We tend to believe that our emotions are reliable indicators of the way things are in the world. How many times have you heard someone say, "I have a good feeling about this"—a college application, a lottery ticket, a new relationship—only to discover that things don't necessarily work out just because we have a good feeling about them? Older relatives are particularly fond of these kinds of pronouncements. "I know you'll do well." "I can't imagine they won't hire you." "I'm sure everything will work out fine." Really? You're sure? What makes you so sure? Just because you happen to like me?

This was exactly Elizabeth's problem, I realized, as *Pride and Prejudice* began. She thought she was right because she *felt* she was right. Mr. Darcy offended her, so he must be a terrible man. Her sister Jane was lovable, so how could anyone not want his friend to marry her? Elizabeth thought she was thinking, but she was really only feeling—resentment, affection, desire—and her great intelligence made her more susceptible to this delusion, not less. Only later did she realize, after the humiliating recognition of her many mistakes, that head and heart can disagree, and that when they do, the head should win.

This was the conflict that Austen expressed in the title of her very first published novel, *Sense and Sensibility,* and embodied in its two main characters. Elinor Dashwood was sensible; her little sister Marianne was full of sensibility or feeling. Early in the book, the two had an argument that laid out the matter very squarely. "I am afraid," Elinor said, rebuking Marianne for having gone about unchaperoned with a young man, "that the pleasantness of an employment does not always evince its propriety." The fact that something feels good, in other words, does not make it right. "On the contrary," Marianne replied, "nothing can be a stronger proof of it . . . if there had been any real impropriety in what I did, I should have been sensible of it at the time, for we always know when we are acting wrong."

We always know when we are acting wrong: how simple life would be if only that were true. Marianne was a romantic, in both senses. She believed that love is more important than anything else, and certainly more important than what her straitlaced older sister thought was proper. And she was also a devotee of the Romantic movement that was sweeping the West in Austen's day. Austen viewed that movement with alarm precisely because of what it said about the proper relationship between feeling and reason. Romanticism taught that society and its conventions are confining and artificial and destructive, and that reason was simply another one of those conventions, not a source of truth. It taught that the real source of truth was Nature, and that if we only followed the nature within us—our spontaneous impulses and feelings—we would be good and happy and free. A romantic is someone who thinks that if their heart is in the right place, it doesn't matter where their brain is. That was what Marianne meant: that our emotions are a moral compass that can never steer us wrong. If something is pleasant, it must be proper. If it feels good, it is good.

In terms of cultural history, Austen was fighting a losing battle. The Romantic idea gave rise to almost all the great art of the last two centuries. It gave us Wordsworth and Byron, Whitman and Thoreau, modern dance, expressionist painting, Beat poetry, and much, much more. It has set the terms for the way we think and feel ever since the time of Austen, and in particular, for the way we think and feel about thinking and feeling. The most important word in popular music today is not "love," it's "I." And the second most important is "wanna." Popular music is one giant shout of desire, one great rallying cry for freedom and pleasure. Pop psychology sends us the same signals, and so does advertising. "Trust your feelings," we are told. "Listen to your heart." "If it feels good, do it."

These can be the right lessons to learn at a certain point in life. They certainly were for me. I grew up in an Orthodox Jewish community: there were a lot of restrictions, a lot of rules. Don't eat pork. Don't play music on the Sabbath. Don't go out with non-Jewish girls. Don't stray outside the bounds of the group. Every action was prescribed by an ancient tradition, every choice circumscribed by the values of a tight-knit community. Keep your head covered. Say your prayers three times a day. Get A's, go to a good college, make your parents proud. Learning that my feelings mattered—learning to figure out what my feelings were in the first place—was extremely liberating as I got older. I needed to realize that I could do what I wanted with my life and that I could do it *just because I wanted to*. Accepting that my emotions were valid and important and morally significant—that they should have a bearing on how I act—was a crucial part, at that point, of growing up.

Some of Austen's heroines had to learn this lesson, too. They were inexperienced and needed to discover their feelings, or they were neglected and needed to stand up for them. But Elizabeth and Emma and Marianne had already figured out how to do those things. They trusted their gut. They listened to their heart. If it felt good, they did it. Their problem, like that of so many young people, was that they had too great a belief in their own feelings. They had achieved the relative autonomy of adolescence—learning to trust yourself—but now they had to take the next step, into the full autonomy of adulthood. They needed to learn to doubt themselves.

And that was what Elizabeth finally did. That was what

happened when she read the letter that overturned her beliefs—
and why she had to read it twice. Its arguments—its infuriat-
ingly rational arguments—flew in the face of her feelings, and
the first time through, her feelings rebelled. But the second
time, her honesty forced her to listen—forced her to *think*. By
telling us Elizabeth's story, I saw, Austen was calling us to do
something very difficult, something that violates our instincts
and intuitions. But of course it does. She was telling us, precisely, to question our instincts and intuitions. She wanted us
to override our emotions, which dwell within us and urge us to
do what we want, and replace them with reason—with logic,
with evidence, with objectivity—which stands outside us and
doesn't care what we want.

Learning this lesson was oddly liberating. Just because I thought
that another person had done something to me, I was now
forced to acknowledge, didn't mean that I was right. I might be
offended by something they had said, but maybe I'd misunder-
stood them. I might be mad because they were getting ugly with
me, but maybe I had started it. Feelings are always *about* something, and that "something" is not itself a feeling. It's an idea,
a perception of a situation, just as Elizabeth's feelings were
based on her perceptions of certain situations. Everyone could
see that Jane loved Bingley; Elizabeth's family wasn't really all
that bad; Mr. Darcy was insufferably proud: these were the perceptions, the ideas, on which her feelings were based, and they
all turned out to be wrong. And because ideas can be wrong,

the emotions that are based on them can also be wrong. So now I had a way to let go of my feelings when they *weren't* legitimate—when they weren't correct. I could acknowledge my emotions, but I didn't have to be controlled by them.

Needless to say, not everybody wants to hear that their feelings aren't necessarily valid. In fact, a lot of people hate Jane Austen for just that reason. They see her as cold and prudish, a schoolmarm and killjoy. In graduate school, we split into two camps over the question—Jane Austen, pro or con—and emotions ran high. At a certain point, we were each expected to teach a class that included one nineteenth-century novel. Now, there are a lot of great nineteenth-century novels, but almost all of us chose one of only two: *Pride and Prejudice* or *Jane Eyre*. It may seem like a small matter, but great issues were felt to be at stake (as they always are in graduate school). The decision wasn't just a pedagogical choice, it was a statement of faith, a declaration of self, for the books represented the strongest possible expressions of two diametrically opposed views of life.

In *Pride and Prejudice,* reason triumphs over feeling and will. In *Jane Eyre,* Charlotte Brontë's own typically Romantic coming-of-age story, emotion and ego overcome all obstacles. Those of us who chose *Pride and Prejudice* couldn't imagine how you could stand to read anything as immature and overwrought as *Jane Eyre*. Those who chose *Jane Eyre* couldn't believe that you would subject your students to something as stuffy and insipid as *Pride and Prejudice*. Our choices, of course, reflected our personalities. The Brontë people, we Austenites

felt, tended to go in for self-dramatization and ideological ex-
tremism. We regarded ourselves as a cooler, more ironic bunch.

Brontë herself, in a letter to a friend, articulated the indictment against her illustrious predecessor:

> *She does her business of delineating the surface of the lives*
> *of genteel English people curiously well; she ruffles her*
> *reader by nothing vehement, disturbs him by nothing pro-*
> *found: the Passions are perfectly unknown to her; she rejects*
> *even a speaking acquaintance with that stormy Sisterhood;*
> *even to the feelings she vouchsafes no more than an occa-*
> *sional graceful but distant recognition. Her business is not*
> *half so much with the human heart as with the human eyes,*
> *mouth, hands and feet; what sees keenly, speaks aptly, moves*
> *flexibly, it suits her to study, but what throbs fast and full,*
> *though hidden, what the blood rushes through—this Miss*
> *Austen ignores.*

But Austen did not ignore the feelings—Elizabeth and her story
were full of them—and she certainly knew about the passions.
Lydia was nothing *but* the passions, and Elizabeth was tossed
by her share as well. "How despicably I have acted!" was not the
declaration of a passionless person. Austen valued the feelings
and passions; she just didn't think we should worship them.

Yet my Brontëan peers rejected the older novelist for a deeper
reason as well, one that Brontë herself would not have understood. To assert that reason should govern emotion is to defy
the modern dogma that the two cannot be disentangled in the

first place. In the past hundred years, Freud and others have brought us to the view that objectivity is an illusion, that our rational conclusions are merely manifestations of hidden impulses or covert expressions of self-interest—above all, when it comes to ideas regarding our own conduct and judgment, which is, of course, what Jane Austen's novels are about.

But Austen didn't buy it. In the letter that changed Elizabeth's mind about everything, her correspondent had this to say about whether Jane had seemed indifferent to Bingley's attentions: "That I was desirous of believing her indifferent is certain—but I will venture to say that my investigations and decisions are not usually influenced by my hopes or fears. I did not believe her to be indifferent because I wished it;—I believed it on impartial conviction." The first half of this, with its smug tone, might strike us as insufferable, and the second might strike us as improbable, but Austen meant us to accept it all. "Impartial conviction"—the ability to think our way above our limited point of view—was a real human possibility for her, and the person who wrote that letter was capable of it. For Elizabeth, growing up meant learning to become capable of it, too.

By making mistakes, and recognizing her mistakes, and testing her impulses against the claims of logic, the heroine of *Pride and Prejudice* learned the most important lesson of all. She learned that she wasn't the center of the universe. Growing up, for her creator, means coming to see yourself from the outside, as one very limited person. This was Austen's vision of redemption, just as the moment of humiliation—that excruciating scene of exposure—was Austen's vision of grace.

In the terms in which both comedies and tragedies have been understood since the time of Aristotle, *Pride and Prejudice* pivoted on a pair of twinned events: a recognition and a reversal. The heroine saw something—about herself, about her actions—and as a result, her fortune changed. But Austen also altered the traditional pattern in an enormously profound way. In the classic comic plot, a pair of young lovers are kept apart by some external obstacle, some "blocking figure" that represents the eternal antagonism of age and youth: a possessive father, a jealous old husband, the laws and customs of an antiquated, repressive society. Austen changed everything by putting that obstacle on the inside. Now we ourselves are the blocking figures who are causing us so much trouble. *We* are the ones standing in the way of our own happiness. Once Elizabeth was ready to be happy, it didn't matter what any of the grown-ups thought. For Austen, reason is liberation, and growing up is the truest freedom of all.

So it was with me. Early that fall, after a summer spent reading like I had a gun to my head and a final night of sleepless terror, I crept into the examination room to face my inquisitors and staggered out two hours later having passed my qualifying exams. Afterward, one of the professors—that Clark Gable lookalike with the cigarette voice—asked me if I had plans to get started on my dissertation.

"I think I need to take it easy for a while," I said.

"That's a good idea," he replied. "You should let your mind lie fallow."

"Lie fallow?" I said. "Lie prostrate."

But the truth is, I did have a plan. After reading my way through Jane Austen's stories about growing up, I decided that the time had come for me to do a little growing up of my own. I could no longer stay in that dingy room, with those random roommates, in that neighborhood where I had spent almost all of my life since I was seventeen. Most importantly, I could no longer live in my father's shadow. A lot of my friends had moved downtown by that point, or out to Brooklyn, and I decided I was going to join them. I would find my own place, I would get some real furniture, and I would finally learn how to live on my own.

My father took me to lunch the next day—at the faculty club this time, by way of celebration. As we ate our baked salmon, I told him about the exam, but the mood turned sour when I explained what I planned to do next. He didn't like it one bit. "It's going to cost you a lot more!" he warned. That wasn't really true. It was going to cost me more, but not a lot more. Besides, his answer was to pull some strings to get me a better place within university housing—rushing in to solve the problem once again, or what he wanted to think was the problem— which would have cost me just as much.

In any case, money wasn't the point. He sensed, even if he couldn't say it, what the real point was. By moving away from the neighborhood, I was moving away from him, and that's exactly what he was trying to head off. Brooklyn? What was Brooklyn? Brooklyn was where he lived when he came over before the war. It was the place you got out of, not the one you went back to. Why would anyone want to move out there?

But I knew why. Moving to Brooklyn might turn out to be a huge mistake, but if so, it was a mistake that I was going to make on my own. I was tired of being infantilized, tired of being afraid: afraid to fail, afraid to disappoint him by failing. I had had enough of our old drama of criticism and defiance, protection and rebellion. I was ready for a new chapter. Like Elizabeth Bennet, I had found my freedom.

CHAPTER 3

northanger abbey
learning to learn

From the beginning, my love for Jane Austen had been intertwined with my love for the professor with whom I had first encountered her. He was the one who had taught the seminar where I read *Emma*, he was the one who had shepherded me through my oral exams, and now he would be the one with whom I would undertake the inconceivable task of writing my dissertation.

But first he did the impossible by helping me find a great, cheap New York apartment. I had been schlepping around the city for weeks on end trying to figure out somewhere to live—filling out forms in shady brokerage offices, answering ads for fifth-floor walk-ups, auditioning for spots as the fourth roommate in apartments the size of a decent bedroom, checking out places where the bathtub was in the kitchen, the kitchen was in the living room, and the living room reeked of rotting fish from the Chinese market downstairs—when he mentioned that his next-door neighbor was looking for someone to rent one of the floors in her brownstone.

The place was a palace compared to the things I'd been look-ing at, and she was asking far less than she could have gotten on the open market, so it was way too sweet a deal for me to worry about the fact that I'd be living right next to the person who'd be supervising my work for the rest of my time in school. I did experience one little wave of panic, though. Smoking pot with some friends a few days after signing the lease, I stumbled into one of those moments of stoned clarity. *Oh, my God!* I thought. *I'm moving in next to my professor! Could there be a more obvious way of telling the entire world—especially my professor—that I think of him as a father substitute?* Nor was the irony of breaking free from one father only to go running into the arms of another in any way lost on me. I could practi-cally feel the diapers growing on me as I sat there. But even in that state, something told me to calm down and stay with my first instinct. I had too much to learn from this man to back away from him now.

He was the youngest old person I had ever met. He was al-ready old enough to retire by the time I took his class, but he was still going stronger than anyone else in the department. He advised a huge number of graduate students, taught courses on a vast range of subjects (nineteenth-century fiction, Romantic poetry, Native American literature, children's literature, science fiction, Great Books, etc., etc.), helped run about eight profes-sional journals, published a new book every three years or so,

and even took on extra classes—an unheard-of thing and a tes-
tament to his incredible devotion as a teacher. A houseguest of
his—a medical student, no layabout herself—once told me that
she'd hear him hustling down the stairs first thing in the morning, getting a running start on his workday before she'd even
had a chance to climb out of bed.

But it wasn't just his energy. He had a young person's ability
to see the world with fresh eyes. His white hair shot up off his
forehead like a jolt of discovery, and when he came across a
new idea, all the lines in his face would stand at attention. He
always wanted to hear what you had to say, no matter how
much you stumbled while trying to say it, because he never
missed an opportunity to learn something new.

It took me a while to figure all this out. In fact, I wondered
at first if I had made a mistake by taking his class. That first
day, as he came bustling into the room with a stack of books
under his arm, a little old man with a white beard, his manner
seemed oddly abrupt, almost jumpy, his eyes kind of squirrelly,
and he gave a sort of chuckle, as if he were enjoying a private
joke that he didn't plan to share with us. He came across as
eccentric, to say the least, if not actually soft in the head, and
the impression was not dispelled by the questions he proceeded
to ask. They seemed absurdly simple—silly, really, almost stupid, too basic and obvious to ask a class of freshmen, let alone
a graduate seminar.

But when we tried to answer them, we discovered that they
were not simple in the least. They were profound, because they
were about all the things we had come to take for granted—

about novels, about language, about reading. Questions like, what does it mean to identify with a literary character? I thought I knew, but did I really? Does it simply mean putting yourself in their place? Obviously not. Or approving of their actions? But we're happy to identify with bad characters, given the right encouragement. No, the best I could come up with was that it seemed to be a kind of in-between state—you're somehow them and not them at the same time—that can't exactly be put into words. Which wasn't really much of an answer at all.

Or again, he observed that there is one part of *Madame Bovary* that no one ever translates into English. Huh? Well, he said, the title—why is that? That one really brought me up short, almost made me angry, it was so audacious. Were you even allowed to ask a thing like that? On the other hand, how *would* you translate it? Lady Bovary? But she's not an aristocrat. Mrs. Bovary? But that's much too plain. The answer seemed to be that there *is* no English equivalent for "*Madame,*" not even "Madam," which said more than I really wanted to know about the differences between the two cultures, and, therefore, my ability to understand the novel altogether.

Within about half an hour, I had started to get what the old man was doing, and I realized that I had never experienced anything like it before. He was stripping the paint off our brains. He was showing us that everything is open to question, especially the things we thought we already knew. He was teaching us to approach the world with curiosity and humility rather than the professional certainty we were all trying so hard to cultivate. In order to answer his questions, we had to forget everything and start over again from the beginning. "Answers are easy," he would later say. "You can go out to the street and any fool will give you answers. The trick is to ask the right questions."

I knew a good thing when I saw one. I took a second class, in Romantic poetry, and became a regular at office hours. It felt like a privilege to be able to sit next to his desk and talk to him one-on-one. He never made us feel like anything less than his equals, even though we weren't. He had an impish laugh, though, and he could be shifty. (When I found out that he also studied Native American literature, I decided that he must be Coyote, the trickster. But we had a tendency to mythologize him. An Indian friend saw him as the elephant-headed god Ganesh, remover of obstacles.) If you said something vague or half-formed, he'd pretend to misunderstand you, as if he were slightly dense, so that by fighting your way back to what you really meant, you'd have to figure out what you'd been trying to say in the first place. I'd catch myself walking out of his office backwards, as if I'd been in the presence of royalty.

My dearest hope, once I started teaching myself, was to have the same kind of impact on my students. Starting our third year, the graduate program required us to teach three years of freshman English. The challenge thrilled me; I had always wanted to be a teacher, and now, after encountering my professor, I was more eager than ever to get into the classroom. But once I did, all the air went out of my balloon, and fast. Something was desperately wrong with what I was trying to do, but

I couldn't figure out what it was. I would come into class with long chains of questions that I had painstakingly designed to lead my students to the ideas I thought they needed to grasp, but they never managed to give me the answers I wanted, and the whole thing would deteriorate into a guessing game.

Instead of being receptive to what I had to tell them, they would fold their arms and sit back in their chairs and stare at me with those skeptical-teenager looks on their faces. The air in the room would go sour, like a bad smell. Time turned to jelly. By about ten minutes in, a little piece of my mind would detach itself and float up to the ceiling, watching me for the rest of the hour as I stood there flailing away. It was like one of those dreams where you find yourself onstage and realize that you've forgotten to learn the lines. I'd rush from class with a guilty feeling in my stomach, like a criminal making a getaway, or try to engage a student as we left the room, hoping for a last-minute reprieve. But of course they couldn't get out of there fast enough.

As for their writing—the thing I was supposed to be helping them get better at—they would hand in little essays twice a week, and I would spend hours covering them with red marks, pouncing on every dangling modifier and misplaced comma like an avenging angel. No matter how bad things were going in the classroom—this was my twisted logic—it was the one thing, I thought, that I could do for them. And then they would hand in the next set of papers, and all the same mistakes would still be there. I wanted to pull my teeth out. Shouldn't they have learned this stuff already? Why weren't they trying harder? Didn't they appreciate what I was doing for them? I wanted to blame them for the way things were going, but I secretly knew that I wasn't the teacher I thought I was going to be, and I certainly wasn't anything like the one my professor was. I began to wonder if my whole desire to go into academia hadn't been a terrible mistake.

Under the circumstances, I was only too happy to turn back to my other work. The first chapter of my dissertation was going to be about Jane Austen, needless to say, and I started out by going back and rereading all of her novels, this time in chronological order. That meant beginning with *Northanger Abbey,* a short, light work whose playfulness and youthful charm had delighted me the first time around but that I hadn't paid a lot of attention to otherwise.

Catherine Morland, the figure at the center of the story, was only seventeen—one of the youngest and certainly the most naïve of Austen's heroines. In fact, she may have been the novelist's own mocking self-portrait. If Austen resembled Elizabeth Bennet as a young woman, Catherine may well have been what she was like as a girl. Both were daughters of clergymen in sleepy country villages. Both came from big families—eight kids in Austen's case, ten in Catherine's—and both had a bunch of older brothers. Catherine, at ten, was a tomboy: "she was moreover noisy and wild, hated confinement and cleanliness, and loved nothing so well in the world as rolling down the green slope at the back of the house"—just the kind of slope the Austens had at the back of their own house.

At fourteen, Catherine preferred "cricket, base ball"—yes,

baseball, and how marvelous it is to imagine the young Jane Austen playing shortstop—"riding on horseback, and running about the country" to reading books. Or at least, serious books. Catherine loved reading novels but hated having to study history—just like her creator, who composed a satirical "History of England" ("by a partial, prejudiced, & ignorant Historian") when she was just about the same age.

But at fifteen, "appearances were mending." Catherine began to curl her hair, long to dance, read love poems, and wear pretty clothes. Her looks improved, and by seventeen she had become an attractive girl. But one thing was missing: her little country neighborhood afforded no young men to arouse her heart. At last, her moment came when she was taken on holiday to Bath, the most fashionable resort in England—a town of theaters and balls, shopping and gossip, grand houses and beautiful views, a place to see and be seen, and the Austen family's favorite vacation spot. Just as the Austens used to stay with Jane's rich aunt and uncle, who went so he could "take the waters" for his gout, Catherine accompanied her neighbors the Allens, the wealthiest family in the district, who went for the same reason.

In Bath, Catherine fell in with two pairs of siblings, each of whom decided to take her in hand and teach her, in very different ways, about life. One pair was John and Isabella Thorpe, vain and knowing young people who stuffed Catherine's head full of false ideas. John was the kind of garrulous, shallow young man that people in Austen's day referred to as a "rattle":

I defy any man in England to make my horse go less than ten miles an hour in harness. . . . Miss Morland; do but look at

my horse; did you ever see an animal so made for speed in
your life? . . . Such true blood! . . .

Look at his forehand; look at his loins; only see how he
moves; that horse cannot go less than ten miles an hour: tie
his legs and he will get on.

John was clearly a fool, but Catherine was so green, and John
was so impressed with himself—she listened to his palaver
"with all the civility and deference of the youthful female mind,
fearful of hazarding an opinion of its own in opposition to that
of a self-assured man"—that she couldn't help letting herself
be taken in.

John, however, was nothing compared to Isabella. He was
merely silly; she was selfish, hypocritical, and cunning. ("'This
is my favourite place,' said she as they sat down on a bench
between the doors, which commanded a tolerable view of everybody entering at either; 'it is so out of the way.'") Isabella,
four years older than Catherine, introduced her protégée to all
the arts of insincerity: how to flirt, how to lie, how to be a
tease. Manipulating her new friend for John's benefit, she did
everything she could to throw Catherine into her brother's
arms. When John offered to take the heroine out alone for a
drive, a highly improper suggestion in those days, his sister
chimed in as if on cue. "'How delightful that will be!' cried
Isabella, turning round. 'My dearest Catherine, I quite envy
you; but I am afraid, brother, you will not have room for a
third.'"

Some of the worst parts of Isabella's influence came from
the kind of books to which she introduced her younger friend.

Northanger Abbey was a satire of the gothic fiction so popular in Austen's day—the exact same stuff she had taken off so raucously in her juvenile sketches. The name was a parody of high-flown titles like *The Mysteries of Udolpho* or *The Castle of Otranto*. (*Northanger* would have been the equivalent of something like *New Jersey.*) Austen herself must have loved those books, in a perverse, guilty-pleasure sort of way. She could never have lampooned them as brilliantly as she did if she hadn't been reading them by the bucketful—and you don't keep reading what you simply despise. But the joke on Catherine was that she believed what she read. Like Isabella's artificial behavior, the extravagant stories of wicked noblemen and haunted castles that the two girls read together—and that Catherine, at least, was innocent enough to take as realistic—gave the heroine all the wrong ideas about the world.

Yet it wasn't just the Thorpes. Catherine's whole environment—a world of polite falsehoods, faked emotions, and empty social rituals—conspired to miseducate her. The night of their arrival in Bath, Mrs. Allen took her young ward to a ball, but since they failed to run into anyone they knew, Catherine was forced to remain without a partner:

> *"How uncomfortable it is," whispered Catherine, "not to have a single acquaintance here!"*
>
> *"Yes, my dear," replied Mrs. Allen, with perfect serenity, "it is very uncomfortable indeed."*

James, Catherine's older brother and John Thorpe's friend from college, showed up in town in time to hear his sister gush about how impressed she was with Isabella. "I am very glad to hear you say so," he responded, having been taken in by her as thoroughly as Catherine had, "she is just the kind of young woman I could wish to see you attached to; she has so much good sense, and is so thoroughly unaffected and amiable." Catherine didn't seem to stand a chance amid this company, and she was soon aping the people around her without even realizing it. Mr. Allen came to collect his wife and charge at the end of that first, disappointing evening:

> "Well, Miss Morland," said he, directly, "I hope you have had an agreeable ball."
>
> "Very agreeable indeed," she replied, vainly endeavouring to hide a great yawn.

Fortunately, Catherine was also befriended by a second brother and sister, Henry and Eleanor Tilney. Henry, who like Isabella Thorpe was a good bit older than the heroine, went about educating her in a completely different way. Clever and animated, he was also so quirky and silly that Catherine did not know what to make of him initially. This was their very first dialogue, after they'd been dancing with each other for a little while:

> "I have hitherto been very remiss, madam, in the proper attentions of a partner here; I have not yet asked you how long you have been in Bath; whether you were ever here before; whether you have been at the Upper Rooms, the theatre, and the concert; and how you like the place altogether. I

*have been very negligent—but are you now at leisure to sat-
isfy me in these particulars? If you are I will begin directly."*

"You need not give yourself that trouble, sir."

*"No trouble, I assure you, madam." Then forming his
features into a set smile, and affectedly softening his voice,
he added, with a simpering air, "Have you been long in Bath,
madam?"*

"About a week, sir," replied Catherine, trying not to laugh.

"Really!" with affected astonishment.

"Why should you be surprised, sir?"

*"Why, indeed!" said he, in his natural tone. "But some
emotion must appear to be raised by your reply, and surprise
is more easily assumed, and not less reasonable than any
other. Now let us go on. . . ."*

Instead of training Catherine to follow the conventions of
life in her society, like Isabella or Mrs. Allen—training her unconsciously, to follow them unconsciously—Henry was trying
to wake her up to them by showing her how absurd they were.
But he didn't do it by being didactic. He did it by provoking
her, taking her by surprise, making her laugh, throwing her off
balance, forcing her to figure out what was going on and what
it meant—getting her to think, not telling her how.

A few days later, the two were dancing together again. John
Thorpe, idly observing the proceedings, sauntered over to Catherine to engage her attention for a couple of minutes of horse-
related prattle (partners would separate and come back together
in the kind of dancing people did in Austen's day), and when
Henry rejoined her, he lodged the following protest:

"I consider a country-dance as an emblem of marriage. Fi-
delity and complaisance are the principal duties of both;
and those men who do not choose to dance or marry them-
selves, have no business with the partners or wives of their
neighbours."

"But they are such very different things!"

"—That you think they cannot be compared together."

"To be sure not. People that marry can never part, but
must go and keep house together. People that dance only
stand opposite each other in a long room for half an
hour." . . .

"In one respect, there certainly is a difference. In mar-
riage, the man is supposed to provide for the support of the
woman, the woman to make the home agreeable to the
man. . . . But in dancing, their duties are exactly changed;
the agreeableness, the compliance are expected from him,
while she furnishes the fan and the lavender water. That, I
suppose, was the difference of duties which struck you, as
rendering the conditions incapable of comparison."

"No, indeed, I never thought of that."

"Then I am quite at a loss."

Now Henry was coming at Catherine from a different direction, and for a different reason. He was still using humor, but
it was a humor of paradox, not imitation, and instead of provoking Catherine to question social conventions, he was asking
her to examine her mental categories, rethink her conceptual
boxes. Marriage is one thing, dancing something else, but are
they really so different? Sort of and sort of not—and Henry

was challenging her to sort out how. The earlier scene had been a performance: he mimicked, she laughed. This one was a dialogue. Now he was inciting her to speak, then pretending to misunderstand her, even at the risk of looking like a dunce, in order to force her to fight her way back to what she meant—and thus, to figure out what she really thought in the first place.

And that's when I realized what I had been looking at the whole time, and what I was doing wrong as a teacher. Sly, impish, ironic, willing to play the fool for the sake of getting someone to think—a little quirky, a little abrupt, but always exciting to talk to: that was Henry Tilney, but it was also my professor. What made my professor such a great teacher was not that he was brilliant, or that he had read everything—though he was, and he had—but that he forced us to think for ourselves, just as Henry did to Catherine, and provoked us to reconsider our assumptions, just as he did to her: all the conventions about what you were supposed to say about a work of literature, all our mental categories for understanding novels and characters and language.

We were ourselves a bunch of Catherines, after all, we graduate students, stepping uncertainly into a new phase of life. No, that actually gives us too much credit. At least Catherine knew that she was naïve, even if she didn't understand just how naïve she was. We were really a bunch of Thorpes, young people coping with feelings of insecurity in an intimidating new world by pretending to know more than we really did, and being rather competitive about it, to boot. My professor was the opposite. He pretended to know less than he did, refused to play the role of wise man or sage. Or rather, he *knew* that he knew less than he did, because he recognized that everything he knew—all his own assumptions and conceptions—was subject to constant reappraisal.

He taught by asking questions, and so did I, but only now did I see how utterly different our questions were. Mine were really only answers in disguise, as if I were hosting some sadistic form of *Jeopardy!* I wasn't a teacher, I was a bully. My *students* were the Catherines, coming to the marvelous world of college, bustling with new sights and possibilities, just as she had come, wide-eyed, to Bath. But I wasn't Henry; I was Isabella. I wasn't helping them; I was manipulating them—and doing so, to a far greater extent than I wanted to admit, in order to gratify my own ego. I *was* telling them what to think, even if, by trying to get them to say it first—that is, by putting words in their mouths—I was pretending not to. I was trying to turn them into little versions of me, instead of better versions of themselves.

When my professor asked a question, it wasn't because he wanted us to get or guess "the" answer; it was because he hadn't figured out an answer yet himself, and genuinely wanted to hear what we had to say. Just so, Henry's whole "dancing equals marriage" thing didn't really have a point, a specific lesson or message. He simply wanted to get Catherine's mind moving so the two of them could have an interesting conversation—a conversation more stimulating than, "Yes, my dear, it is very uncomfortable indeed," or "This is my favourite place; it is so out of the way," or "I defy any man in England to make my horse go less than ten miles an hour." A conversation in which both he and she had a chance to actually learn something, and so in which a real mental—and therefore emotional—connection between them could be made.

My professor was like Henry, but of course, as I quickly realized, they were both like Henry's creator. Playful, impish, provoking: this was Austen exactly, and never more so than in *Northanger Abbey*. Austen used the novel to make us *her* students. Henry was her surrogate, and Catherine was ours, and she went about teaching just the way that he did. In fact, she taught, in part, through him. Everything he said to Catherine she was also necessarily saying to us. When Henry ridiculed the conventions of polite chatter, it was the empty gestures of our own conversations that we inevitably thought of. When he rearranged Catherine's mental categories, it was our sluggish ideas that started to wake up and stir.

But she also did far more than that. Henry taught, in that first scene, through impersonation. He pretended to become someone else—set smile, softened voice, simpering air—and proceeded to act that character out in a way that revealed the character's folly to Catherine, his audience. Austen did not pretend to become someone else, but she certainly did impersonate any number of characters. "Yes, my dear" and "This is my favourite place" and "I defy any man in England": these were the equivalents of Henry's "Have you been long in Bath, madam?"—satiric performances meant to call our attention to behavior we normally take for granted. Austen, like Henry, taught by showing—which means, by arousing. By putting something in front of us and expecting us to think about it.

She wrote novels, not essays, and more than just about any other author, she refused to mar her novels by putting essays into them. She never lectured, never explained: never interrupted her stories to hold forth on what she wanted us to think they meant, or deliver her opinions on the state of the world. She also never tampered with her characters by putting her own ideas into their mouths. Writing to her sister, Cassandra, upon the publication of *Pride and Prejudice,* she sketched out her philosophy about these matters, albeit in the ironically inverted way in which her letters often spoke of serious things. "The work is rather too light & bright & sparkling," she now professed to think about the novel, "—it wants to be stretched out here & there with a long Chapter—of sense if it could be had, if not of solemn specious nonsense—about something unconnected with the story; an Essay on Writing, a critique on Walter Scott, or the history of Buonaparte." A cackle of authorial delight, followed by a glance at the degenerate practices of lesser novelists.

Austen was never didactic, and she didn't like didactic people, either. In *Pride and Prejudice,* Mary Bennet was fond of quoting heavy books, and Mr. Collins was fond of reading them aloud, and both of them were held up as fools. Henry never "told" Catherine anything—except once, and then Austen gently laughed at him, too. He and Catherine and his sister, Eleanor, who had also befriended the heroine, were taking a walk to the top of a hill overlooking the town of Bath. The Tilneys, "viewing the country with the eyes of persons accustomed to drawing," were soon deciding "on its capability of being formed into pictures." Austen was referring here to the contemporary vogue for the "picturesque," landscapes that conformed to a certain idea of visual beauty: moody skies, gnarled trees, ruined shacks, and so forth, all arranged according to the laws of pictorial art. But Catherine knew nothing of this, so Henry was only too happy to fill her in:

> She confessed and lamented her want of knowledge, declared that she would give anything in the world to be able to draw; and a lecture on the picturesque immediately followed, in which his instructions were so clear that she soon began to see beauty in everything admired by him, and her attention was so earnest that he became perfectly satisfied of her having a great deal of natural taste. He talked of foregrounds, distances, and second distances—side-screens and perspectives—lights and shades; and Catherine was so hopeful a scholar that when they gained the top of Beechen Cliff, she voluntarily rejected the whole city of Bath as unworthy to make part of a landscape.

In fact, as we know from her family, Austen was a great devotee of the picturesque herself, just as she loved the gothic novel. But she understood that any art or idea or pattern of behavior, left unexamined, hardens into cliché. Once you begin taking it too seriously, you're only a step away from taking yourself too seriously, and before you know it, you start to sound like Mr. Collins, "lecturing" and "instructing" instead of laughing and surprising. Your students, in turn, their minds improved by your enlightened guidance—"she voluntarily rejected the whole city of Bath as unworthy to make part of a landscape"—start talking nonsense.

Now I understood why the novel had to begin in the odd way that it did. "No one who had ever seen Catherine Morland in her infancy," the first sentence read, "would have supposed her born to be an heroine." The line was a joke about the conventions of gothic fiction, one that the rest of the first chapter went on to elaborate. Catherine's father "was not in the least addicted to locking up his daughters," "there was not one family among their acquaintance who had reared and supported a boy accidentally found at their door," and so forth. That much was obvious. But now I realized that the first sentence was also a way of calling attention to the fact that this novel, too, would necessarily trade in conventions. A heroine and a romance, a Mr. Wrong and a Mr. Right, perils and misunderstandings, conflicts and complications, revelations and reversals, and at last, a happy ending: these were the conventions that Austen herself employed in every one of her novels, and she could not have done without them any more than a detective novelist can do without a corpse. Yet she didn't want us to get sucked in by her conventions, either—didn't want us to let ourselves be lulled into the trance of gullibility that readers are always falling into, mistaking an artificial version of reality for the genuine article. Stay awake, Austen was telling us. Don't take things for granted, not even the things I'm telling you myself.

. . .

In other words, pay attention. And pay attention, above all, to
your own feelings, because the world is always trying to get you
to lie to yourself about them. "'Very agreeable indeed,' she replied, vainly endeavouring to hide a great yawn." Our feelings,
Austen was saying, are sometimes impolite and often inconvenient for the people around us. Friends and relatives are apt to
tell us, instead, what we *should* be feeling—what we supposedly *are* feeling—if only to make their own lives easier or more
exciting. This was Isabella, talking to Catherine about Henry,
whom at that point the heroine had met only once:

> *"Nay, I cannot blame you. . . . Where the heart is really at-
> tached, I know very well how little one can be pleased with
> the attention of anybody else. Everything is so insipid, so
> uninteresting, that does not relate to the beloved object! I
> can perfectly comprehend your feelings."*
>
> *"But you should not persuade me that I think so very much
> about Mr. Tilney, for perhaps I may never see him again."*
>
> *"Not see him again! My dearest creature, do not talk of
> it. I am sure you would be miserable if you thought so!"*

Isabella, remember, was the one who had introduced the heroine to all those romantic novels. She wanted her friend's life
(her own, in other words, by proxy) to be full of the same extravagant emotions she had been reading about, even if they
ended up making Catherine unhappy—or rather, especially if
they did.

But Henry behaved in exactly the opposite fashion. In a scene much later in the novel that Austen made a point of pairing with this one, Henry and Catherine conducted the same kind of dialogue about Isabella herself. By this time, Isabella had shown her true colors as the false schemer she really was, and the girls' friendship was at an end:

> *"You feel, I suppose, that in losing Isabella, you lose half yourself: you feel a void in your heart which nothing else can occupy. . . . You feel that you have no longer any friend to whom you can speak with unreserve, on whose regard you can place dependence, or whose counsel, in any difficulty, you could rely on. You feel all this?"*
>
> *"No," said Catherine, after a few moments' reflection, "I do not—ought I? To say the truth, though I am hurt and grieved, that I cannot still love her, that I am never to hear from her, perhaps never to see her again, I do not feel so very, very much afflicted as one would have thought."*

Henry was drawing on the same pool of emotional clichés that Isabella had—for there were clichés about friendship as well as romance then, in life as in art, in life because of art, just as there are today (the "frenemy," the "bromance," the "BFF"). But instead of telling Catherine what she must have been feeling, he simply asked her to pay attention to what she actually was feeling. And by that point in the novel, with his help, she had learned to do exactly that.

"You feel, as you always do," he now replied, "what is most to the credit of human nature. Such feelings ought to be investigated, that they may know themselves." In *Pride and Prejudice,* Elizabeth had learned to put thinking above feeling, and so did I, by reading about her. Now I learned a more complex idea about the relationship between the two. It is good to be in touch with your feelings, but it is even better if you also think about them. Feelings, Austen was saying, are the primary way we know about the world—the human world, anyway, the social world, the people around us. They are what we start with, when it comes to making our ethical judgments and choices.

Catherine had registered a new understanding of Isabella, but she had registered it, at first, deep down in her gut. Now, by investigating those feelings, she brought that recognition to the level of consciousness. A few pages later, when Isabella tried, with a fawning letter, to crawl back into her friend's good graces, the heroine was ready. "Such a strain of shallow artifice could not impose even upon Catherine," Austen told us. "Its inconsistencies, contradictions, and falsehood struck her from the very first. She was ashamed of Isabella, and ashamed of having ever loved her."

All this chimed with something that my professor had been trying to teach me ever since I had first encountered him, though he had never come right out and said it. One of the most shocking things about his courses was what they *didn't* involve. The rituals of the graduate seminar, all of them devised to turn us into professional scholars, were entirely absent. No lists of secondary sources or packets of supplemental reading, no theoretical frameworks or critical jargon. No seminar papers, either, even though they were supposed to be the principal means by which we received our training: twenty-page essays, complete with footnotes and a bibliography, our first baby steps in writing for professional publication. Instead, he simply wanted us to write a one-page paper every week. *One* page, with no citations and no outside reading. Just you and the book and one of those fiendishly simple questions he liked to ask.

Literary study, he was trying to tell us, was not about learning a secret language or mastering a bag of theoretical tricks. It was not about inventing a new, professional personality, either. It was about getting back in touch with the ways we used to read—the ways people read when they're reading for fun—but also about intensifying them, making them more thoughtful and deeply informed. "Such feelings ought to be investigated, that they may know themselves." It was about trusting our responses, but examining them, too.

Feelings are also the primary way we know about novels—which, after all, are training grounds for responding to the world, imaginative sanctuaries in which to hone and test our ethical judgments and choices. Our feelings are what novelists work with, the colors on their palette. What was it if not my feelings that Austen had been working with in *Emma*, when she taught me about boredom, or *Pride and Prejudice*, when she taught me about certainty? Curiosity, perplexity, exhilaration; the buzz in the brain, the tumult in the soul—that, my professor was telling me, was what I had to work with; that was where my scholarship should start. With the love of reading that had gotten me to graduate school in the first place.

.   .   .

The ways we *used* to read. One of the things that *Northanger Abbey* taught me, one of the things that both my professor and Austen understood, is how hard it is to see what's right in front of us, even when we think we're looking. Catherine was not un-educated before Henry got to her; she was something worse: thanks to Isabella and Mrs. Allen and everyone else, she was miseducated.

That was the point of the scene on Beechen Cliff, Henry's own moment as a bad teacher. There, Catherine really did begin in a state of ignorance, *un*educated ("She knew nothing of drawing—nothing of taste"), and by the time her teacher was done, she couldn't see a thing. She could see foregrounds and distances and second distances, side-screens, perspectives, lights, and shades—everything the theory of the picturesque told her she was supposed to see—but she missed the entire city of Bath, couldn't recognize what might be beautiful about it.

That was just a warm-up, though, for the heroine's visit, later in the novel, to Northanger Abbey itself, the Tilney family's rambling old Gothic estate. Having read all those novels with Isabella—*The Castle of Wolfenbach* and *The Necromancer of the Black Forest, Horrid Mysteries* and *The Midnight Bell*—Catherine thought she knew what she was going to find there. Sure enough, alone in her room on her first, blustery night, nerves on edge for every sign of a secret door, every sound of a creaking board or rattling chain, she came upon a strange old cabinet that looked like just the kind of thing to conceal a few horrid mysteries of its own:

Catherine's heart beat quick, but her courage did not fail her. With a cheek flushed by hope, and an eye straining with curiosity, her fingers grasped the handle of a drawer and drew it forth. It was entirely empty. With less alarm and greater eagerness she seized a second, a third, a fourth; each was equally empty. . . . The place in the middle alone remained now unexplored. . . . It was some time however before she could unfasten the door . . . but at length it did open; and not vain, as hitherto, was her search; her quick eyes directly fell on a roll of paper pushed back into the further part of the cavity, apparently for concealment, and her feelings at that moment were indescribable. Her heart fluttered, her knees trembled, and her cheeks grew pale. She seized, with an unsteady hand, the precious manuscript.

A dark house, a stormy night, a cryptic roll of paper—all her expectations seemed to be coming true:

The manuscript so wonderfully found, . . . how was it to be accounted for? What could it contain? To whom could it relate? By what means could it have been so long concealed? And how singularly strange that it should fall to her lot to discover it! Her greedy eye glanced rapidly over a page. She started at its import. Could it be possible, or did not her senses play her false? No, they did not. The precious manuscript turned out to be nothing other than—a laundry list.

And that was only the beginning. One dose of reality was not enough to cure Catherine of her imaginative projections, and before she knew it, she had concocted an elaborate fantasy about buried secrets and violent crimes in the Tilney household. In fact, something scary truly was going on at Northanger Abbey—Catherine was right to detect a dark cloud hanging over the family—but the violence was emotional, not physical. Catherine missed it—until, before long, she was blindsided by it—because she was looking, all too zealously, in the wrong direction. Her fantasies were not just foolish, they were dangerous. Long passageways and old cabinets notwithstanding, there really was nothing remotely mysterious about Northanger Abbey. The only thing separating Catherine from the truth was her own mind.

We may be born with an untrained eye, Austen was telling us, but by the time we get to be Catherine's age—by the time we're old enough for college, let alone graduate school—our eyes have been trained only too well. That, I now understood, was why my professor needed to ask us all those "irritating" questions, as he liked to put it. It wasn't enough for him to be receptive to what we had to say, or to treat us like equals. In fact, that kind of teaching has been very much in vogue of late: encourage students to express themselves, validate their ideas, pass out the positive comments like lollipops.

But students don't come to school with open minds, they come with all the concepts they've already acquired ("foregrounds, distances, and second distances . . ."), and they can't wait to project them onto everything they read. If you're in college, you go hunting for "symbolism" or "foreshadowing" or "Christ figures." If you're in graduate school, it's "constructions of otherness" or "discourses of sexuality" or "the circulation of power." Either way, you end up like Catherine, with a very elaborate theory that bears no relationship to what's actually going on in front of you. Henry challenged Catherine; my professor challenged his students; Austen challenged all of us. The job of a teacher, I now understood, is neither to affirm your students' notions nor to fill them with your own. The job is to free them from both.

My professor taught novels, and Catherine was mistaught by them, but neither he nor Austen was finally concerned with novels as such. Learning to read, they both knew, means learning to live. Keeping your eyes open when you're looking at a book is just a way of teaching yourself to keep them open all the time. Now I understood how my professor had managed to stay so young. He never settled into certainty, never stopped challenging himself—and getting us to challenge him—as hard as he challenged us. There was a paradox, I realized, at the heart of Austen's work. She showed us how to grow up, but she also wanted us to remain young. Her heroines became adults, but her adults, by and large, did not look very good at all. Here was Catherine and her chaperone on a slow morning in Bath:

> She sat quietly down to her book after breakfast; . . . from habitude very little incommoded by the remarks and ejaculations of Mrs. Allen, whose vacancy of mind and incapacity for thinking were such, that as she never talked a great deal, so she could never be entirely silent.

Mrs. Allen was a warning to Catherine, sitting there all too absorbed in her book, but even more, she was a warning to us. Be careful, Austen was saying. Don't end up like that.

Austen loved youth, precisely because it is the time of life when we are most open to new experiences. Her great subject was change, and young people still retain the capacity for change. Her novels, charged with the energy of youth, quick-sighted and playful, were full of young people and their concerns—the adults often relegated, like parents in a *Peanuts* cartoon (or Mrs. Allen on that morning in Bath), to the inaudible margins. *Pride and Prejudice*, I realized, had only eight adult characters and fully twenty-one younger ones, starting with the five Bennet girls. *Northanger Abbey*, a story on a smaller scale, had seven young people and only two adults who played any kind of significant role. Adults are boring, Austen seemed to feel—or at least, they all too often let themselves become so.

As her letters to her nieces and nephews make clear, Austen celebrated youth in her life as well as in her books. She was always looking to entertain and engage her young relations, always interested in what they had to say. When her brother Frank took his new bride to visit their older brother Edward's estate, Austen composed a poem for Edward's daughter Fanny, then thirteen, imagining how the exciting new experience must have felt from her perspective. When her brother James's daughter Caroline acquired a niece of her own at the ripe old age of ten, Aunt Jane entered into her feelings, too. "Now that you are become an Aunt," she wrote, "you are a person of some consequence & must excite great Interest whatever You do. I have always maintained the importance of Aunts as much as possible, & I am sure of your doing the same now."

She encouraged, but she never condescended. Three of her brothers' children tried their hands at writing novels—inspired, no doubt, by their famous aunt's success—and Austen would return their drafts with detailed criticism as well as praise. Even one of Caroline's stories, sent when she was nine, was taken seriously enough to critique:

> I wish I could finish Stories as fast as you can.—I am much obliged to you for the sight of Olivia, & think you have done for her very well; but the good for nothing Father, who was the real author of all her Faults & Sufferings, should not escape unpunished.

Fanny and Anna, her oldest nieces, became her closest correspondents in the last years of her life (both were twenty-four at the time of Austen's death), but little Caroline, only twelve when her aunt passed away, became a regular one, too, and the letters Austen sent her during those last months were remarkable for the maturity they grant their recipient and the genuine pleasure their writer obviously took in the relationship. As for Fanny, around the same time, a series of personal reflections she'd sent her aunt elicited this:

> You are inimitable, irresistible. You are the delight of my Life. Such Letters, such entertaining Letters as you have

lately sent!—Such a description of your queer little heart! . . .
You are the Paragon of all that is Silly & Sensible, common-
place & eccentric, Sad & Lively, Provoking & Interesting.

She might have been talking about Catherine Morland, and the same vitality, and joy in vitality, shines through her responses to both young women. Finally, there was the letter she sent one January to her brother Charles's daughter Cassy, also nine at the time, in which every word was spelled backwards, a missive that began, "Ym raed Yssac, I hsiw uoy a yppah wen raey," and ended, "Ruoy Etanoitceffa Tnua, Enaj Netsua." No wonder Tnua Enaj was the favorite of her many nieces and nephews.

Austen's work contained a paradox, yet it didn't have to be a tragedy. You can get older, she was telling me, but still remain young. That, I started to realize, was part of what had been keeping me from growing up for all those years, the fear of foreclosing possibilities, of turning into another boring adult with a spouse and a house. Now I was getting a new idea about what life can have in store.

Once I moved in next to my professor, I found myself running into him from time to time outside our buildings. He had a long-term project to repaint the railings in front of his house (he and his wife would go away for the summers, so the progress was slow), and we would stand there now and then—I'd have a backpack, he'd be holding a brush—and talk about whatever happened to be on my mind. One day it was *Northanger Abbey*, and he called my attention to a scene I hadn't thought about before.

"It's the one where Catherine tells Henry, 'I have just learnt to love a hyacinth'," he said. "Now that's exceedingly interesting, don't you think?"

"Uh, I guess so," I said—not an unusual response on my part.

"Well," he went on, "Austen is saying that we need to *learn* to love things, that it doesn't just happen by itself. That's not an obvious idea."

"No, I guess not," I said. "Love is supposed to be completely spontaneous and natural, like love at first sight."

"Right," he said, "but the most remarkable thing is, we *can* learn. And think about what Henry says in response." He could apparently recite the scene from memory, but I needed a little help.

"'Who can tell,'" he quoted, "'the sentiment once raised, but you may in time come to love a rose? . . . The mere habit of learning to love is the thing.'"

The habit of learning: if Catherine could learn to love a hyacinth when she was seventeen, my professor was telling me—or rather, Austen was telling me, through my professor—I could keep learning to love new things my whole life. Of course, it was my professor himself who had helped me learn to love Jane Austen in the first place, against expectations at least as stubborn as the ones that Catherine brought to Northanger Abbey. But I was starting to get it now: the wonderful thing about life, if you live it right, is that it keeps taking you by surprise. Just when you think that nothing can be more uninteresting than a hyacinth (or a scene about a hyacinth, or an author who writes scenes about hyacinths), you find it becoming a new source of delight.

Catherine thought she saw things at Northanger Abbey that weren't really there, but the novel, my professor explained, was not against imagination. Quite the opposite. It was against delusion, against projection, against thinking the same old thing again and again, whether it's the idea that all balls are "very agreeable indeed" or that all old houses conceal dark secrets. True imagination, he went on, means the ability to envision new possibilities, for life as well as art. Mrs. Allen and the rest of Austen's dull adults were not ignorant or stupid so much as they were unimaginative. Nothing was ever going to change for them, because they couldn't imagine that anything ever would.

But Austen's ideas about staying young contained a further paradox. When I went back and looked up that scene for myself, I remembered *how* Catherine had learned to love a hyacinth. "Your sister taught me," she said to Henry. "I cannot tell how. Mrs. Allen used to take pains, year after year, to make me like them; but I never could, till I saw them the other day in Milsom Street." Young people, Austen was saying, need to *learn* to be young, must be woken up to the world's physical beauty (the loveliness of hyacinths) as well as to their own moral beauty (their capacity to love them). They need to be taught, somehow, by older people, people who have learned it already—people like the Tilneys, or my professor, or Jane Austen. Taught by example ("I cannot tell how"), not the pedantic taking of pains we can too well imagine Mrs. Allen having employed.

The need for teachers: there is something in the modern spirit that bridles at the notion. It seems inegalitarian, undemocratic. It injures our self-esteem, the idea of having to confess our incompleteness and submerge our ego beneath another person. It outrages our Romantic temper, which feels that the self is autonomous and the self is supreme. And if the teacher is a man and the student a woman, as they are in *Northanger Abbey*— and, even worse, an older man and a younger woman—it offends our feminist sensibilities, as well.

But Austen accepted it, even celebrated it. Nearly all of her heroines have teachers of one kind or another, and in her own life, we know, her mentors were many and crucial. There was James, her oldest brother, ten years older, who had, according to his son James-Edward, Austen's first biographer, "a large share in directing her reading and forming her taste." There was Eliza Capot de Feuillide, her glamorous cousin, fourteen years her senior, who became Jane's friend and idol when she descended upon the Austens from France. There was Anne Lefroy, the wife of a neighboring parson when Austen was a girl—beautiful, spirited, clever, a great reader and wit—her "best loved and admired mentor," according to Austen biographer Claire Tomalin, a kind of "ideal parent" to whom she could turn for advice and encouragement. And finally, there was Cassandra herself, Austen's deeply beloved older sister, about whom she would speak "even in the maturity of her powers," as James-Edward put it, "as of one wiser and better than herself."

My professor and I were having another one of those conversations when the subject turned to Austen again, her ideas about mentors and maturation. "Austen is saying that it's important to spend time with extraordinary people," he said with a twinkle in his eye. "So that's what I advise you to do: spend time with extraordinary people."

I had come to graduate school with a very different idea about what it means to get an education. It was an idea that derived from my father. Here was a man who had earned three university degrees, spoke six languages, and had taught himself all about classical music and European art and Western history— a man who equated being educated with knowing things, knowing facts. And the purpose of knowing things, in a strangely circular way, was simply to "be" educated, to be able to pride yourself on being a "man of culture" (and feel superior to those who weren't). Knowledge, culture, ego. Mine was a household, growing up, where it was understood that there were certain things one "ought to know," where "having heard of" Brahms or Giotto was considered a virtue in itself—even if one didn't know any more about them than that one was a composer, the other a painter—and where one encounter was considered equivalent to "knowing" (or as my father would have put it, "being acquainted with") a work of art.

My father had never been very keen on literature—it was just stories, after all; he preferred books that gave you real information—but he began to show an interest once I started graduate school, as a way of sharing the experience. When I took a course on Ben Jonson, he read a biography of the playwright, though not any of his actual plays. When I took a course on Shakespeare, I suggested that he might at least try some of those. "I've read them already," he said. "When I was in my twenties." And indeed he had, by buying a *Complete Works*, starting at the beginning, and reading until he had gotten to the end. Another "ought to know" checked off the list.

Knowledge, culture, ego. Even if my notion of what it meant to know a work of art or literature had become more strenuous than my father's, that was still pretty much the formula I was working with until well into my time in graduate school—as my freshman English students, not to mention the woman I was in love with the summer that I studied for my orals, as well as the one I was going out with when I first read *Emma*, could readily attest. But now I was learning a new idea, and learning it with the help of that other "father," the one I'd been so nervous about getting too close to when I took him up on the apartment. It was a new idea about education, but it was also a new idea about being a man—"of culture" or otherwise. You didn't have to be certain, I now saw, to be strong, and you didn't have to dominate people to earn their respect. Real men weren't afraid to admit that they still had things to learn—not even from a woman.

For it was Austen, of course, who had ultimately taught me these new ideas about knowledge and education. While she had no patience with ignorance and valued characters who had "information" and "conversation"—people who knew what was going on in the world and could talk about it intelligently—she ridiculed the emphasis, in both the education of children and the self-education of adults, on the mere acquisition of facts. Elizabeth Bennet's sister Mary wasn't just pedantic; she was also dense.

"What say you, Mary?" her father teased her at one point.

> *"For you are a young lady of deep reflection, I know, and read great books and make extracts."*
>
> *Mary wished to say something very sensible, but knew not how.*

As for formal education as it existed in Austen's day—of which there was in any case precious little to be had by girls—she had this to say in a short poem titled "On the Universities":

> No wonder that Oxford and Cambridge profound
> In Learning and Science so greatly abound
> Since some *carry* thither a little each day
> And we meet with so few that *bring any away.*

When Cassandra visited some friends at a nearby estate, her sister included this bit of invective in one of her letters:

> *Ladies who read those enormous great stupid thick Quarto Volumes, which one always sees in the Breakfast parlour there, must be acquainted with everything in the World.—I*

detest a Quarto.—Capt. Pasley's Book is too good for their
Society. They will not understand a Man who condenses his
Thoughts into an Octavo.

Quartos were large-format volumes reserved for books that took themselves very seriously; octavos were half the size and much less pretentious. As for Captain Pasley's work, *Essay on the Military Policy and Institutions of the British Empire*, Austen called it "a book which I protested against at first, but which upon trial I find delightfully written & highly entertaining"— evidence both that she was no stranger to serious works of nonfiction and that she judged whether a book was likely to tell her anything valuable by the way it was written. Her problem with quartos was not their subject matter but their ponderous prose, their "thickness" in both senses.

Of course, the kind of books she valued most were novels. This was not a fashionable position—novels were considered too trivial and feminine—but she defended it without apology. Writing to Cassandra about a new library that was about to open in the neighborhood (libraries were private businesses at the time and charged a subscription fee), she noted that:

As an inducement to subscribe Mrs. Martin tells us that her
Collection is not to consist only of Novels, but of every kind
of Literature etc. etc.—She might have spared this pretension
to our family, who are great Novel-readers & not ashamed
of being so;—but it was necessary I suppose to the self-
consequence of half her Subscribers.

In *Northanger Abbey*, a novel about reading novels, John Thorpe marked himself out as just such a snob when Catherine asked if he had read *The Mysteries of Udolpho*: "Udolpho! Oh, Lord! Not I; I never read novels; I have something else to do."

It was a response that Austen had already taught us to disdain. She was not against *Udolpho* and its kin; she was only against the way that people misread them. And just to make sure that we didn't miss the point, she made this thundering declaration very early in the book, right after telling us that Catherine read novels herself:

> *Yes, novels; for I will not adopt that ungenerous and impolitic custom so common with novel-writers, of degrading by their contemptuous censure the very performances, to the number of which they are themselves adding—joining with their greatest enemies in bestowing the harshest epithets on such works, and scarcely ever permitting them to be read by their own heroine, who, if she accidentally take up a novel, is sure to turn over its insipid pages with disgust. . . . There seems almost a general wish of decrying the capacity and undervaluing the labour of the novelist, and of slighting the performances which have only genius, wit, and taste to recommend them. "I am no novel-reader—I seldom look into novels—Do not imagine that I often read novels—It is really very well for a novel." Such is the common cant. "And what are you reading, Miss ——?" "Oh! It is only a novel!" replies the young lady, while she lays down her book with affected indifference, or momentary shame. "It is only Cecilia, or Camilla, or Belinda"; or, in short, only some work in which the*

greatest powers of the mind are displayed, in which the most
thorough knowledge of human nature, the happiest delinea-
tion of its varieties, the liveliest effusions of wit and humour,
are conveyed to the world in the best-chosen language.

So there. As for history, the ultimate in "serious" reading, this was how Catherine, explaining why she hated it, described what it involved: "The quarrels of popes and kings, with wars or pestilences, in every page; the men all so good for nothing, and hardly any women at all." It was a great line, that second half, but Austen also intended something deeper by it, a sly reference to her own project. "Hardly any women at all": in other words—since women had essentially no role in public affairs—nothing about private life, nothing about personal life. Whereas the novel, the great genre of private life, was almost always, in Austen's day, about women and almost always by them—two of the main reasons that people were so quick to put it down.

Histories tell us what happened, but novels can teach us something even more important: what might happen. The opening line of *Northanger Abbey* was a joke about gothic fiction and a way of calling attention to Austen's own use of conventions, but it was also, I now saw, something still more. "No one who had ever seen Catherine Morland in her infancy, would have supposed her born to be an heroine." From the humblest beginnings, the greatest possibilities. Catherine never did become a traditional heroine, never did have the wild passions and epic adventures that we're supposed to find so admirable. Instead, she became something better.

By waking up to the world, by renouncing certainty and cynicism, by opening herself to new experiences—all of which take real courage, real strength—she turned her life into an adventure that would never end. This, Austen told us, is the true heroism. Life, if you live it right, keeps surprising you, and the thing that keeps surprising you the most, I now understood, is yourself. The caterpillar can't imagine the butterfly, the child can't imagine the adult, and no one, before they do it, can imagine what it feels like to fall in love. We can never reach the end of what's inside us, never know the limit of our own potential.

These were lessons to explore for a lifetime, but the first place I applied them was the classroom. Instead of thinking of a session as a kind of engineering problem—how to transfer a certain quantity of material from my head to my students'—I started to see it as an opportunity to incite them to discover the powers that were waiting, unborn, within them, and in doing so take both themselves and me by surprise. I went from feeling that a good class was one in which I had "gotten my points across" to regarding it as one in which I had learned something myself—not because my learning was the goal, but because if I had found out something new, it meant that I had given my students the freedom to think their way beyond me.

All of a sudden, teaching became a joyful experience. I arrived in the classroom with excitement and left it with exhilaration. The time in between, which now seemed as if it was never long enough, began to feel like a collaboration, even an adventure—like I was working a trapeze, and the best moments came when I let go of the bar, let go of my plan, and just flew through the air, confident that someone would be there on the other side to catch me. It was scary, but it was also really fun.

I began to like my students rather than resent them. They suddenly seemed really smart and interesting—because I was letting them be, instead of having to suppress their talents in order to maintain my fragile sense of intellectual authority. They seemed to start to like me, too, began to come to talk to me, even confide in me. Best of all, a few of them became my friends, in that special way that can happen between a student and a teacher—the way that had happened between me and that extraordinary person whom I felt so privileged to live next door to.

It turned out that I hadn't made a mistake by wanting to become a professor, after all. It had just taken me a while to discover my potential. I had started to learn how to teach—but more importantly, after more than twenty years in school, I had finally learned how to learn.

CHAPTER 4

mansfield park
being good

That first year in Brooklyn, I sensed my life beginning to grow into a new shape. It was the first time I had had a place of my own, and I could almost feel my arms and legs getting longer with all the psychological space I had to move around in. I got a platform for my futon, bought a nice set of chairs at a stoop sale down the street, even picked up some plants and learned how to keep them alive. (When I asked the clerk at the garden store if my potting soil would go bad if I didn't, you know, use it up right away, he said, "You wanna know if this *dirt* is going to get *stale*? I feel like I'm talking to my little brother!") My English-muffin-pizza days were over. Instead, I picked up *The New Basics Cookbook* and started having people over for things like minty roasted potatoes and lemon-garlic-rosemary chicken. A few months in, I even acquired a cat—this was some serious responsibility now—a little gray thing who needed a home and who took to curling up beside me on my desk while I was working.

Living so far from Columbia, I began to see less of my graduate school friends. Instead, I gravitated toward a very different world. Another friend had become involved with a woman who'd been raised on the Upper East Side and gone to a fancy Manhattan private school. Her prep-school crowd was back in the city after college, dabbling in this or that and living the high life, and these were the people I started spending time around. It would have been hard not to. This was the upper crust, the world of Edith Wharton or F. Scott Fitzgerald updated for the nineties: posh, polished young people who gave off a glow of glamour and sophistication that drew me like a moth. I was dazzled, I was seduced. It was an undreamed-of world of privilege, and I was grateful just to be able to watch.

There was the stunning department-store heiress who ran a chic East Village café and went out with a guy who talked about getting into film. There was the scion of a consumer-products fortune who had married his art-school girlfriend. There was the lovely, blue-eyed daughter of an Ivy League president. And there was one young woman who seemed to be richer than all the others put together—even they grumbled when she took us to a "little place around the corner" where the desserts started at twelve dollars—and who had picked up a tall, Dutch, model-beautiful boyfriend somewhere along the way.

I went to their openings and partied with them afterward in downtown lofts. I partook of artful brunches and elegant candlelit dinners at a town house in Cobble Hill. I was ushered into the large East Side apartment building where my friend's girlfriend grew up, to discover that there were only two doors facing us when the elevator opened: one for her apartment and one for the other one. I spent weekends at her family's summerhouse on Long Island, with four or five bedrooms and a swimming pool and a lawn that rolled down about three hundred feet to the sound.

Here it was, I thought, that fabulous, glamorous New York world that I had always sensed around me but had never known how to get to. The city is Oz when you grow up, as I had, in the Jersey suburbs, a shining mirage in the distance, and ten years of living there had never really changed that. I could walk the streets and hit the bars on a thousand college nights; I could eat black bean cakes in Chinatown, blini in Brighton Beach, and bowls of flaczki at Christine's; I could discover the Kitchen, the Knitting Factory, and P.S. 122; but I could never shake the feeling that I was still just wandering somewhere out there in the cold. The real city, as I imagined it, the magic kingdom where beautiful people in shining clothes said clever things in darkened rooms, still lay there on the other side of the velvet ropes.

But now I felt like I'd been slipped a pass, even if it was strictly limited-access. My friend's girlfriend befriended me— she turned out to be a tremendously magnetic personality, a great storyteller and reader of character—but the rest of them mostly ignored me. I could hardly blame them. I didn't know how to dress, where to stand, how to order a drink or cross a room at a party. So I stayed on the edges, gazed at the women, and tried to pay for my keep with witty remarks. Yet still I hoped to find a place within the circle, if only by special dispensation. I would become the house intellectual, I imagined, prized for my ability to spice up a gathering with a dash of literary zest. The guys would respect me; the women would notice me. Eventually, one of them—it almost didn't matter which—would find me intriguing enough to make me her boyfriend.

It wasn't always easy, after one of those weekends or one of those nights, to go back to plugging away at my Austen chapter. It was the longest of long slogs, writing a dissertation, and I had still only barely begun, and I often wondered where it would finally get me, whether there would be a job out there at the end of it all. Sometimes I even lost patience with Austen herself—specifically, when I thought about *Mansfield Park*. I had read it a couple of times by then, and I still could not see anything to like about the book, or comprehend how she had ever written it. The novel seemed to pit itself against everything Austen believed in, everything that was delightful about *Emma* and *Pride and Prejudice* and *Northanger Abbey*—against wit and energy and curiosity. Its mood was dour, even bitter, its view of life crabbed and prudish.

Worst of all, it forced me to keep company with an exceptionally unappealing heroine. Fanny Price was a poor little girl who had been adopted into her rich uncle's family at the age of ten. Terrified by the grandeur of her new surroundings at Mansfield Park and awed by a foursome of confident, attractive older cousins, Fanny developed into a meek, weak adolescent, frail in body and poor of spirit. She had nothing of

Emma's self-confidence, or Elizabeth's sense of fun, or Catherine Morland's openness to life, no capacity whatsoever for happiness or joy.

Her passivity may have been understandable given the circumstances, but it seemed to conceal something more like passive aggression. When her cousins and some friends decided to put on a play for their own amusement—exactly the kind of thing, by the way, that the Austens did all the time when Jane was growing up—Fanny refused to take part in so supposedly improper a scheme. But it wasn't enough for her just to stay out of it. She couldn't stand the idea that anyone else might be having a good time:

> *Everybody around her was gay and busy, prosperous and important; each had their object of interest, their part, their dress, their favourite scene, their friends and confederates: all were finding employment in consultations and comparisons, or diversion in the playful conceits they suggested. She alone was sad and insignificant: she had no share in anything; she might go or stay; she might be in the midst of their noise, or retreat from it, . . . without being seen or missed.*

To which I felt like saying, "Too bad." But self-pity was not enough for her. That was already her default mode, a "Don't worry about me, I'll just sit in the dark" kind of martyrdom. No, as she crept around watching the rehearsals, "Fanny believed herself to derive as much innocent enjoyment from the play as any of them." "Innocent enjoyment": the very note of defensive hypocrisy. She got pleasure from the play, and then she got some extra pleasure from condemning it.

Fanny was already eighteen by then, but she still seemed like a child, willfully stuck in the same place she had been when she'd first arrived at Mansfield Park. Indeed, the so-called East room, her own little domain on an upper floor, had once served as the family schoolroom, and it retained its childish furniture even now. "Innocent" was right. Fanny's problem with the play, after all, a romance called *Lovers' Vows*, was the covert opportunity it afforded her cousins and their friends for flirting with one another. Prim, proper, priggish, prudish, puritanical, Fanny simply couldn't deal with the threat of adult sexuality. And to top it off, she didn't even like to read novels. Too racy for her, no doubt, and certainly too frivolous.

On the other hand, no one else at Mansfield Park was any better, and most of them were a lot worse. Fanny, at least, had the virtues of her faults. If she was self-pitying, she was also self-sacrificing. If she was passive, she was also patient, generous, and uncomplaining. But the rest of the household was mainly different flavors of awful. Sir Thomas Bertram, Fanny's uncle, was a distant, overbearing patriarch whose presence sat on Mansfield like an oppressive weight. (Only his absence overseas made the thought of the play possible.) Lady Bertram, his indolent trophy wife—"a woman who spent her days in sitting, nicely dressed, on a sofa, doing some long piece of needlework, . . . thinking more of her pug than her children"— was as lovely, energetic, and intelligent as an expensive throw pillow.

Maria and Julia, the Bertram daughters, were slick and spoiled. ("Their vanity was in such good order," Austen told us, "that they seemed to be quite free from it.") Tom, the older son, was an irresponsible playboy. And then there was Mrs. Norris, Lady Bertram's sister, probably the most repulsive character in all of Austen: spiteful, miserly, and mean as dirt, a woman who reacted to the death of her husband "by considering that she could do very well without him" and who harried Fanny—"Remember, wherever you are, you must be the lowest and last"—like a wicked stepmother. But indeed the whole family treated the heroine like a glorified servant—that is, when they bothered to notice her at all.

The whole family but one. Edmund, the kind, attentive younger son, was an oasis of decency in a desert of selfishness. But even he was hard for me to take—as proper and priggish as Fanny herself, and in fact, as her mentor and adored older cousin, the one primarily responsible for making her that way. Nor was Edmund any less immune to the lures of hypocrisy. He, too, opposed the play—until he saw the chance to do a little flirting of his own. Not that he regarded it like that, of course. The cast was one short, and Edmund only took the unclaimed part to forestall the greater impropriety of having to give it to someone outside the family circle. It also just happened to involve playing opposite a young woman in whom by then he had developed a somewhat more than innocent interest.

For a new pair of young people had arrived upon the scene. Henry and Mary Crawford, whose half sister was the wife of the Mansfield clergyman, were everything, it seemed to me, that the novel had been needing, a gust of fresh air from beyond the musty confines of Mansfield Park. Henry was dashing and debonair, a sophisticate, a raconteur, a man of the world—cleverer than Tom, more confident than Edmund, and a lot more fun than either one. As for his "remarkably pretty" sister—healthy and high-spirited; witty, playful, and independent—she reminded me of no one so much as Elizabeth Bennet. "I am very strong," Mary said, bouncing off a horse. "Nothing ever fatigues me but doing what I do not like." She even came with an extra little dash of sauciness. Henry and Mary had been raised by their uncle, a high-ranking naval officer. "My home at my uncle's brought me acquainted with a circle of admirals," she quipped at one point; "Of *Rears,* and *Vices,* I saw enough"—a naughty pun on military ranks and the sexual reputation of the Royal Navy.

The Crawfords were independently wealthy, and their money gave them a freedom of spirit that was previously unknown to the heavy atmosphere of Mansfield Park. Their arrival jolted both the Bertram siblings and the novel itself awake. Walks, rides, outings, the play—suddenly it was all liveliness and movement. Of course, Fanny herself was appalled. These were not her kind of people, or her idea of how to pass the time (which tended to involve a lot of sitting). And when Mary and Edmund began to take a shine to one another—his steadiness of character attracting her almost against her will—the heroine was thrown into a panic of jealousy.

But if she stewed with secret spite, Mary treated her with a gentle consideration that seemed to flow from real goodwill.

"I am not going to urge her," Mrs. Norris barked in front of everyone when Fanny refused to participate in the play, "but I shall think her a very obstinate, ungrateful girl; . . . very ungrateful, indeed, considering who and what she is":

> Edmund was too angry to speak; but Miss Crawford, looking for a moment with astonished eyes at Mrs. Norris, and then at Fanny, whose tears were beginning to shew themselves, immediately said, with some keenness, "I do not like my situation: this place is too hot for me," and moved away her chair to the opposite side of the table, close to Fanny, saying to her, in a kind, low whisper, as she placed herself, "Never mind, my dear Miss Price, this is a cross evening: everybody is cross and teasing, but do not let us mind them."

As for Henry, a hardened flirt, he was tougher to like, luring Maria Bertram's affections, during the time of the play, from the rich but dull-witted young man to whom the oldest Mansfield girl was already engaged—though with no motive more serious, on Henry's part, than the gratification of his own vanity. Fanny's turn was next—he boasted to his sister that he only wanted to make "a small hole" in the heroine's heart—but he soon discovered that the influence was running the other way. Like Mary with Edmund, Henry was surprised to find himself susceptible to Fanny's finer, quieter qualities. And as he set out to court her in earnest, he began to display some rather fine qualities of his own: patience and tact and sensitivity, a cultivated mind and a susceptible heart.

As *Pride and Prejudice* ultimately arranged a merging of its hero's and heroine's best qualities, a purging of their faults, so I always rooted, each time I read the novel, for a synthesis of Mansfield and Crawford: Edmund and Fanny on the one hand, Mary and Henry on the other. Goodness matched with boldness, stability with spirit. The cousins would grow up, the siblings would settle down. Everybody would be better, and everybody would be happy.

But then, something happened to change my mind, not only about *Mansfield Park* but also about myself. A year or so after I'd begun to hang around the private-school crowd, my friend and his girlfriend got married. It was more like a coronation than a wedding: a rehearsal dinner the night before at an elegant restaurant overlooking the East River, a stately ceremony in the grand space of an East Side Episcopal church, and an opulent, impeccably tasteful reception at a private club nearby. I fished my best shoes out from the back of the closet and bought my first new suit since my bar mitzvah. Hundreds of people attended, most of them from the bride's parents' rarefied sphere of business associates and social contacts. And then, as I was watching the dancing with some of the other single guys—the department-store heiress was wearing a little black dress with a fur-trimmed neckline that none of us could take our eyes off—one of them said, apropos the groom, "Well, he got what he wanted."

"What do you mean?" I said, looking over to where the newly married man, a big grin on his face, was shaking hands with some of his father-in-law's friends—cool, confident men who looked like they knew where all the levers were. "He's on the inside," came the reply. "He's been working on this for years." My friend, it was true, was not of that world. He had grown up in the South, a professional's son but the grandson of a state trooper, and his mother had been a stewardess. He had gradually worked his way up the chain of academic prestige, through college and graduate school, always traveling in a northeasterly direction, then came to the city, moving from job to job in the same fashion. But I had never imagined that the whole thing had been so calculated.

Sure, I knew in a theoretical sense that people sometimes married for money. I had read *The Great Gatsby* and understood about coming to New York to bury your past and bluff your way into high society. But I had never dreamed that any of those things applied to my friends. Didn't we all just go out with people because we liked them? Weren't we going to marry for love? A phrase popped into my head, understood as if for the first time: "social climber." And then I remembered something that my friend had said not long after I had met his girlfriend. The two of them had wanted to set me up with one of those old schoolmates of hers, but they had had their reservations. "She's high-maintenance," they said. "What's high-maintenance?" I asked. (I hadn't seen *When Harry Met Sally . . .* yet.) "High-maintenance is the worst," my friend said, searching for a way to express the true awfulness of the concept. "It's worse than being ugly. It's worse than being poor!"

It's funny how that hadn't really hit me at the time—or had, but I had let it go. They were such a fun couple, and they promised so much fun to come. I hadn't wanted to hear what he was really saying, or maybe I couldn't quite believe it. But now, at the wedding, seeing the whole world they'd introduced me to spread out in front of me, seeing its logic laid bare, I was forced to think about what it all meant—the greed beneath the elegance, the cruelty behind the glow—and more to the point, what I myself had been doing in it. Because if my friend was a social climber, then what the hell was I? I had never planned things out the way that he had, or even thought about where it was all heading, but my attraction to that golden crowd, my ache to be accepted by them, what did it amount to if not the very same thing? Who was I becoming? Who had I already become?

I'd like to be able to say that I turned my back on that world that very night, but it wasn't so simple. The newlyweds were still my friends, and I didn't find it easy, in any case, to walk away from something that seductive. But I did start to notice all kinds of things—how these people treated others, but also what they did to themselves—that I hadn't wanted to see before. And it wasn't long before I realized, as I returned to my dissertation, that someone had already told me everything I needed to know about that world before I'd even encountered it, only I hadn't been able to listen. For where was I, I finally saw, but smack in the middle of a Jane Austen novel—and one of them, in fact, in particular? What was that realm of luxury and cruelty, glamour and greed, coldness and fun, if not a modern-day version of *Mansfield Park*?

The recognition almost knocked me down. However much I had learned from Austen about myself, I had never dreamed that our worlds bore much resemblance to each other. I lived in a democracy, she lived in an aristocracy. In my world, people could make their way through talent and hard work; in hers, you were pretty much stuck where you were born. In our day, people married for love (or so I had thought). In hers, marrying for money and status was more or less taken for granted. But now I saw how similar our worlds really were, especially at the level where I currently found myself. Beneath the ideals, which looked so different, the very same attitudes: the same values, the same motives, the same ambitions. Whatever I might have wanted to believe, I realized, we also have an aristocracy in this country, and I was looking at it. So in the months that followed the wedding, as I continued to travel within that world—but now more cautiously, more consciously—a process of mutual illumination began to unfold. *Mansfield Park* taught me about my experiences, and my experiences taught me about *Mansfield Park*.

Who was I, ultimately, among those rich Manhattanites, if not another Fanny Price: an outsider, an onlooker—creeping, largely unregarded, along the edges? What an idiot I had been to think that I could ever really belong, and how pathetic to imagine that my education, of all things, would win me a glamorous girlfriend. That the novel expended so much energy on a play—one that its golden youth put on by themselves, for themselves—made perfect sense to me now. The episode simply made visible what had always been true, that Fanny was and only ever could be a spectator. She may have chosen to sit out the play, but the larger drama of money and status that was being enacted around her all the time—the balls and the games, the flirtation and the matchmaking—she had no more choice to sit and watch than I. We didn't know the lines, and no one would have given us a part even if we had managed to learn them. The play's title, *Lovers' Vows,* was perfectly chosen. Fanny was penniless; at that point in the novel (Henry's later interest was something of a miracle on Austen's part), she wasn't going to find herself reciting those anytime soon.

I also began to understand the unique role that Mansfield itself played in the book. The novel was not the only one of Austen's that was named after a place, but no other place achieved the kind of presence in its novel that this one did. None of her other stories dwelled so insistently within the confines of a single estate. Mansfield was mentioned in the first sentence, and it was named again in the very last line. We discovered its routines, learned the names of its servants, were shown the sources of its wealth. We acquired a sense of its spaces with a richness of detail that was otherwise unknown in Austen's work: the drawing room, where the family gathered; the billiard room, where the young people set up their theater; the East room, where Fanny went to lick her wounds; the gardens; the stables; the parsonage; the park. No wonder the novel was named for the estate. Mansfield Park was a more important character than anyone else besides the heroine.

As for why this should be true, I had only to think of the place that I had come to as a seventeen-year-old suburban boy. Mansfield was for Fanny what New York was for me: a place of awe, astonishment, intimidation, and social peril, a labyrinth of mysterious values and of spaces heavy with symbolic and emotional meaning. About Longbourn, where Elizabeth Bennett grew up, or Hartfield, where Emma lived, we learned almost nothing, and just because those heroines could take their homes for granted. If *Mansfield Park* had been narrated from the perspective of Edmund, say, the estate would have figured as an equally neutral backdrop.

But the novel sees with Fanny's eyes, wide with provincial wonder. Nothing about Mansfield could ever be neutral for her; nothing would ever be taken for granted. The book was about her encounter with the place as much as it was about anything else. Mansfield was a character in the novel for the same reason that New York was in so many movies and television shows—*Taxi Driver, Annie Hall, Sex and the City.* The two places were not just locations: they were climates, moods, cultures. They made their own weather, dictated their terms.

Which made the Bertrams and Crawfords I knew, children of Manhattan, all the more powerful to me. Coming from the magic place, they carried, quite apart from their own beauty or poise, the dazzle of its aura. So too, in the novel, did the Crawfords, who represented something even more than Mansfield: London, the place where they'd grown up, New York's forerunner and equivalent. The Bertrams themselves were provincial compared to them, and it was the glamour of London, I now understood, that the Crawfords sailed into Mansfield on the wind of. It was the source of their worldliness, their knowingness, their confidence.

When the young people, at one point in the novel, were discussing the "improvement" of estates—renovation, in our language, a fashionable subject at the time—Mary delivered her opinion with urban nonchalance. "Had I a place of my own in the country, I should be most thankful to any Mr. Repton [a famous landscape designer] who would undertake it, and give me as much beauty as he could for my money; and I should never look at it till it was complete." Beauty for money: Mary was not just advertising her wealth, she was displaying an ostentatiously metropolitan insouciance in the way she handled it. People in London, she was saying, don't dirty their hands with the details. They snap their fingers, and the world jumps.

Was Mary being a snob? Maybe a little. Mainly she was doing what she always did. She was being charming. Only now did I realize, though, what "being charming" meant. Charming, after all, is a verb—an action, not merely a state. Mary wasn't charming the way that Elizabeth Bennet and Catherine Morland were—unconsciously, as a simple outgrowth of their personalities. She deliberately set out to win people over. It was a performance, I saw, an act. (And the significance of the play, the brilliance of placing it at the center of the novel, was once again brought home to me: these people were already acting all the time.) The idea was counterintuitive. Why would someone who was so much more fabulous than you were bother to prove—to you, of all people, the toad, the provincial—just how fabulous they were? Because they needed to know that *you* thought they were fabulous. Apparently, no matter how poised and confident they seemed to be, they weren't sufficiently convinced of it themselves.

Mary, I realized, was exactly, almost eerily, like my friend's new wife. I had been utterly charmed from the night I had met her—by her stories, by her repartee, by her sense of daring and fun—but only now, thinking back to that encounter, did I see how calculated the whole thing must have been. Of course I'd been charmed: that's what she did. And then it hit me. My friend's wife had done to me exactly what the Crawfords did to the people at Mansfield, but also what they did to us.

And so I finally began to recognize the depth of Austen's cunning in *Mansfield Park*. As Mary seduced Edmund and Henry seduced Fanny, their creator was seeing to it that they were also both seducing the reader. The fact that I had been so taken with them was not the novel's flaw, as if Austen had created characters that she couldn't control; it was, precisely, its strategy. She had done it again, just as she had in *Emma* and *Pride and Prejudice*: orchestrated my responses to teach me a lesson about my responses. She *wanted* me to fall for the Crawfords, and then she wanted me to figure out why. Only this time, it had taken me a lot longer to catch on.

My friend's wife had had a particular reason for wanting to win me over that night—I was her new boyfriend's friend—but as I began to see, she didn't need a particular reason. In a coincidence that was almost too beautiful, she was an actress herself—or had been, in college, before she gave it up, as she once told me, because "the best I was probably ever going to do was shampoo commercials." Instead, she went to law school, or as she put it, "I figured I'd get much better parts as a lawyer than I ever would as an actress." If she boasted about the way she could work a party, she also bragged about her skill at working on a jury, getting them to think exactly what she wanted.

Like the Crawfords, she pushed people's buttons for the simple pleasure of being able to do so, and the challenge of figuring out how. Mary, too, was an acute reader of people. Or as Edmund gushed to Fanny, "I know nobody who distinguishes characters better. . . . She certainly understands *you;* . . . and with regard to some others, I can perceive, from occasional lively hints . . . that she could define *many* as accurately, did not delicacy forbid it." In the case of my friend's wife—or my friend, for that matter, an equally cutting observer—delicacy most certainly did not forbid it, and they had long been regaling me with reflections on the rest of the private-school crowd, from "high-maintenance" to the notion that the twelve-dollar-dessert woman had acquired her gorgeous boyfriend "like she was buying a pretty book." Only now did I begin to wonder, though, what the two of them must have been saying about me, to everyone else, and how they must have been working on *my* buttons, too, without my having realized it.

It was the same in *Mansfield Park*. When Mary comforted the heroine after that vicious attack by Mrs. Norris, I now saw, she may have been motivated mainly by kindness—"the really good feelings by which she was almost purely governed," as Austen slyly put it—but she was also manipulating two people at once. She knew that the way to get to Edmund's heart was to go through Fanny, and that the way to get to Fanny's was by asking her about her brother William, a sailor, the one member of the heroine's original family to whom she remained attached. And indeed, as Mary went on to ask about him, and express her curiosity to see him, and "imagined him a very fine young man," Fanny "could not help admitting it to be very agreeable flattery, or help listening, and answering with more animation than she had intended."

Mission accomplished. But then, Mary was a serial manipulator. She manipulated Sir Thomas, she manipulated Lady Bertram, she even manipulated, for no conceivable purpose, Mrs. Norris. But the novel's greatest symphony of button pushing was Henry's attack on the heroine. As he told his sister:

> I do not quite know what to make of Miss Fanny. . . . Is she solemn? Is she queer? Is she prudish? . . . I never was so long in company with a girl in my life, trying to entertain her, and succeed so ill! . . . I must try to get the better of this. Her looks say, "I will not like you, I am determined not to like you"; and I say she shall.

And when his sister tried to warn him away from hurting so fragile a creature, he protested:

> No, I will not do her any harm, dear little soul! I only want her to look kindly on me, to give me smiles as well as blushes, to keep a chair for me by herself wherever we are, and be all animation when I take it and talk to her; to think as I think, be interested in all my possessions and pleasures, try to keep

me longer at Mansfield, and feel when I go away that she
shall be never happy again.

The speech itself was a little masterpiece of manipulation,
disguising its intentions as it led us along step by step until we
wound up somewhere that we never meant to be.

Did Henry ever really fall for Fanny, later in the novel? I was
sure that he thought he did, but now I wondered what she really
meant to someone like him, or, as a friend, to someone like his
sister. "Give me as much beauty as he could for my money":
the Crawfords were accustomed to traveling in a world of objects made for them to purchase and enjoy, and it occurred to
me that they were used to treating people the same way. The
rich Manhattan kids I knew, of course, were not any different.
"Like she was buying a pretty book": not a kind remark, but
an accurate one.

The idea was made more chilling by the sort of beauty that
Henry now wished to buy. Fanny had grown into a pretty girl,
but what really hooked him was the sight of her reunion, a
couple of months after the play, with that same brother William whom Mary had asked her about. "The glow of Fanny's
cheek, the brightness of her eye, the deep interest, the absorbed
attention. . . . It was a picture which Henry Crawford had
moral taste enough to value." "Moral taste": what a perfectly
slimy phrase that was, the most important matters of character
reduced to the status of a fine wine or toothsome dish, to be
bought, sold, swallowed, and judged.

More than the values I discovered beneath the veneer, more than the certainty that my character was being treated to the same kind of vivisection that I witnessed happening to others', it was that sense of objectification that really began to sour me on my friends and their world. For I had started to realize that I was being treated the same way. Not only were my friends tremendously entertaining people, they gave you the unmistakable impression that they expected to be tremendously entertained—that like Henry, who had "a great dislike" "to anything like a permanence of abode, or limitation of society," they wouldn't tolerate a moment's boredom. And so—it seemed so odd, after all the time we'd spent together—it began to dawn on me that I had never really been able to relax around them, would feel as if I'd been holding my breath the whole time whenever I was in their company. I realized that I always felt as though I had to be *on*—had to be forever ready with a witty remark or a funny story.

My dating life, with all its perils and pratfalls, became a series of comic vignettes retold for their amusement—which was fine, to a certain extent, because it took away the sting of romantic disappointment, but it also never allowed for any real commiseration or shared feeling. It's true that I colluded, unconsciously, in my own objectification, wanted to play the raconteur when I saw that it would let me keep a place at the table, but it's not as if there'd really been a choice. These were not people you wanted to be vulnerable around (they'd probably start calling you "high-maintenance" behind your back), or even just flat in an ordinary way. In fact, since weeks would sometimes go by when I wouldn't hear from them at all,

I started to feel as if I was being treated like a toy: picked up and played with when they wanted whatever it was they thought I had to offer, then dropped again whenever they got bored.

It was just the same in *Mansfield Park*—as Mary implied when Henry first told her about his designs on the heroine's heart. Maria Bertram had finally married her wealthy oaf, and her sister Julia, Henry's first conquest at Mansfield, had gone with them on the honeymoon (as was not unusual in Austen's day). "You ought to be satisfied with her two cousins," Mary told her brother about Fanny, but "the truth is, . . . you must have a somebody. . . . If you do set about a flirtation with her, you never will persuade me . . . that it proceeds from anything but your own idleness and folly." Fanny, for Henry, was nothing more than a hobby at this point, something to do when he wasn't riding or shooting. Or as he put it himself, "How do you think I mean to amuse myself, on the days that I do not hunt?"

The Bertrams, the Crawfords—why did Austen say such terrible things about the aristocracy, if that was the class she came from and loved so much? Because she didn't, on either count. Contrary to popular belief, she was neither an aristocrat herself nor, as her books made perfectly clear—*Mansfield Park* above all—did she even much like the aristocracy. Her heroines, while sometimes rich, were never the richest characters in their books, and they usually didn't marry the richest ones, either, who were generally rather vile—and the richer they were, the viler they tended to be.

As for Austen herself, her father was a clergyman, and most

of her other connections—uncles, brothers, family friends— were clergymen, lawyers, or military officers: gentlemen, yes, but certainly not aristocrats. The Austens were comfortable, but they were far from rich and very far from being, like the families she wrote about, either landed or titled. The Bertrams would have condescended to mix with them, if at all, only in the most distant way—at best, an occasional invitation to a ball, in company with the rest of the district's respectable families.

While Elizabeth Bennet and her sisters were exempt from household responsibilities, and of course Lady Bertram and her daughters were far above anything but the kind of elegant needlework that gentlewomen used to pass the time, Jane and her sister, Cassandra, as girls, had a full roster of household chores: making clothes for themselves and their father and brothers; helping their mother in the kitchen, dairy, garden, and poultry yard (baking bread, brewing beer, boiling jams and jellies); and even picking up a rake when it was time to make the hay.

After the Reverend Austen died, when Jane was twenty-nine, she and her sister inherited, not the thousand pounds the Bennet girls could each look forward to, and certainly not the twenty thousand that Mary Crawford already possessed, but absolutely nothing at all. Everything they had, they were dependent for on others, meaning their mother, who had little enough of her own, or their other family connections—the most important reason they and Mrs. Austen, together with yet a fourth woman, shared a modest house, provided by a relative, to the end of Austen's life.

Short of marriage or inheritance—and finding a husband itself depended on having property to offer—women simply had very few ways of supporting themselves in Austen's day. "Single Women," as she reminded a niece, "have a dreadful propensity for being poor." The most common alternative for a young woman of Austen's class was to become a governess in someone else's family, a condition that *Emma*'s Jane Fairfax, staring down its barrel, equated with slavery. The money that Austen was finally able to make from her novels, the first of which was not published until she was thirty-five—£140 from *Sense and Sensibility*, £110 from *Pride and Prejudice*—was cherished to the last penny. "Tho' I like praise as well as anybody," she once said, "I like what Edward calls *Pewter* too." She didn't just write for the fun of it.

But though Austen neither came from the aristocracy nor entered it, luck gave her a front-row seat for observing its ways. That same Edward, her third brother, had the immense good fortune to be adopted by distant relations, a wealthy, childless couple whose property he inherited and whose name, Knight, he took. Edward's story may well have given his sister the idea for *Mansfield Park*, especially since his oldest daughter, the novelist's favorite niece—eighteen, like Fanny Price, when Austen started to write the novel—was also named Fanny. But if Edward contributed the idea of adoption, and Fanny Knight donated her name, the heroine's experiences—exclusion, alienation, subordination—belonged to none other than Austen herself.

While she visited her brother's estate of Godmersham Park any number of times, and struck up that friendship with Fanny Knight, she was never regarded there as anything more than a poor relation. Like Fanny Price at Mansfield Park, or me in that circle of rich New Yorkers, she remained an outsider, and an inferior. The fault was not Edward's, by all accounts an impeccably generous man (it was he who lent the house, on land attached to yet another one of his estates, in which the Austen women settled after the death of Jane's father). The fault was not even his wife's, though when it came to summoning a spinster sister-in-law to help with her many lyings-in (she had eleven children altogether), she much preferred Cassandra. According to a different niece, "a little talent went a long way with the Goodenstone Bridgeses," Edward's wife's family, "& much must have gone a long way too far."

No, the fault was simply the system's. Austen was treated like an inferior despite being such a close relation, and despite her immense gifts of character and mind, because according to the way that people thought at the time, that was exactly what she was. Fanny Knight herself, over fifty years after Austen's death and nearly as many since she had become a titled lady in her own right, put the matter with brutal frankness. Her aunt, she remembered, "was not so *refined* as she ought to have been from her *talent*." The Austens as a whole, she continued, "were not rich & the people around with whom they chiefly mixed, were not at all high bred, or in short anything more than *mediocre* & *they* of course tho' superior in *mental powers* & *cultivation* were on the same level as far as refinement goes." Cassandra and Jane, she went on, "were brought up in the most complete ignorance of the World & its ways (I mean as to fashion etc.) & if it had not been for Papa's marriage, . . . they

would have been, tho' not less clever and agreeable in themselves, very much below par as to good Society & its ways."

And this, remember, was Austen's favorite niece. She wasn't
being mean; she was being honest. This was simply how people
thought in "Society," in "the World." Family was all well and
good, but it was no substitute for "refinement" or "fashion" or
being "high bred." Cassandra went to help her pregnant sister-
in-law with a willing heart, no doubt, but it wasn't as if she
really had a choice. Edward lent his mother and sisters a house
with an equally good will, but that made them no less his de-
pendents. It is no wonder that the closest friend that Austen
made at Godmersham—a relationship that lasted the rest of
her life—was none other than the family governess: someone
equally marginal, inferior, and dependent. And it is also no
wonder that she used her lifetime of stealthy observation there
to create her cutting portraits of aristocrats like the Bertrams
and the Crawfords.

For all that Austen helped me see about the ways the rich and
wellborn deal with other people—as objects or instruments, as
puppets or toys—her deepest lessons about the dangers of
power and luxury had to do with how such people hurt themselves. It's no fun to have friends who constantly want you to
entertain them, but it's far worse if you're the one who constantly needs to be entertained. The Crawfords' mobility, which
looked so much at first like energy—Mary galloping about the
countryside, Henry dashing about the country—was little

more, I finally saw, than restless discontent. Mary was moping one showery day at the Mansfield parsonage, her half-sister and brother-in-law's house—"contemplating the dismal rain in a very desponding state of mind, sighing over the ruin of all her plan of exercise for that morning, and of every chance of seeing a single creature beyond themselves for the next twenty-four hours"—when a very wet Fanny was spotted nearby and asked to come inside.

"The blessing of something fresh to see and think of was thus extended to Miss Crawford," Austen commented, "and might carry on her spirits to the period of dressing and dinner." The moment went by quickly, but what an indictment it was. So poor was Mary in any kind of inner resources, Austen was telling us, any ability to dwell in her own mind—to read, to draw, or simply to sit still and think—that her spirits couldn't survive a few hours alone indoors. Perpetual amusement, the privilege of the idle rich, leads only, it seems, to the perpetual threat of boredom.

Being able to get whatever you want, Austen was showing me, leaves you awfully unhappy when you cannot get what you want. While the Crawfords' arrival set Mansfield awhirl with schemes of pleasure—the play, a trip to Maria Bertram's fiancé's estate—they always seemed to have a way of going sour. Everyone fought about who was going to get the best parts in the play or the best seats in the carriage, who was going have the chance to flirt with whom. Everyone fought, in other words, over what kind of pleasure they were each going to have, and who was going to have the most.

When Mary's harp arrived from London in the middle of the harvest, she couldn't understand why she found it so difficult to hire a cart to bring it from the nearby town:

> *I was astonished to find what a piece of work was made of it! To want a horse and cart in the country seemed impossible, so I told my maid to speak for one directly; and as I cannot look out of my dressing-closet without seeing one farmyard, nor walk in the shrubbery without passing another, I thought it would be only ask and have. . . . Guess my surprise, when I found that I had been asking the most unreasonable, most impossible thing in the world; had offended all the farmers, all the labourers, all the hay in the parish!*

Charmingly put, as always, but the meaning was clear enough. "I told my maid to speak for one directly": Mary was not accustomed to waiting for a bunch of farmers, and she did not intend to become accustomed to it, either. Like her brother, or most of the Bertrams, she was not the kind of person who was used to hearing "no."

Edmund—who, as a younger son, had to find a way to make a living—planned to become a clergyman. William, Fanny's brother, was already on his way to becoming a naval officer. But Tom, the oldest son—he wasn't going to become anything. He was an heir, after all; he felt himself to be born "only for expense and enjoyment." And Henry Crawford, what were his plans? Like a lot of the wealthy young people I knew—the café-owning heiress, who later took an unsuccessful stab at law school, or her boyfriend, the film dabbler—Henry was a dilettante.

When Edmund talked of his future, Henry imagined how splendid it would be to deliver a sermon. "But then," he added, "I must have a London audience. I could not preach but to the educated. . . . And I do not know that I should be fond of preaching often." When William, Fanny Price's sailor brother, recounted his stories of adventure, Henry wished that he had joined the navy. "He longed to have been at sea," as Austen put it, "and seen and done and suffered as much." The wording was perfect. Henry wished, not to *be* at sea, but to *have been*— to have gotten his suffering over with and now stand ready to reap the credit. "The glory of heroism, of usefulness, of exertion, of endurance, made his own habits of selfish indulgence appear in shameful contrast; and he wished he had been a William Price, distinguishing himself and working his way to fortune and consequence!"

The wish, however, was short-lived. Why work hard if you don't have to? Why restrict your freedom if you have all the money in the world? Henry wanted to do a little of everything but not too much of anything, and so in the end he did precisely nothing. It was not an uncommon predicament among the rich kids I knew, both in that private-school circle and through other connections. Many were chronically aimless, and some were downright miserable, psychologically crushed by the fact that nothing was ever going to be expected of them. At the highest levels of wealth, I heard, doing well meant no more than not having tried to kill yourself. It made me wonder whether people would ever seek to make themselves rich in the first place, if they knew what it was going to do to their children.

The Crawford worldliness, which had always so impressed me, now seemed, in fact, a kind of narrowness. Mary's crack about the hay, her inability to understand that there might be other priorities than the ones that prevail in London, was evidence not only of a bloated sense of entitlement, but also of the special kind of provincialism that belongs to people who think of themselves as cosmopolitan. Once I realized this, I began to see it all around me, including—or especially—coming out of my own mouth. At least people from smaller places recognize that there are other things out there in the world. But if you live in "the center of the universe"—London in Austen's day or New York in ours—then nothing else exists. How could you ever want to spend a day outside the city? Why would you even bother with people who live somewhere else?

Before the business with the hay, Mary had also had some trouble hearing that her harp had arrived at the nearby town in the first place:

> The truth is, that our inquiries were too direct; we sent a servant, we went ourselves: this will not do seventy miles from London; but this morning we heard of it in the right way. It was seen by some farmer, and he told the miller, and the miller told the butcher, and the butcher's son-in-law left word at the shop.

It was like those jokes that New Yorkers make about the pizza in Chicago, or the culture in Los Angeles, or those quaint, slow-witted people that they meet on vacation in Vermont.

More than snobbery, I saw, this was an appalling lack of curiosity. Accustomed to a world of "ask and have," of trading money for pleasure in coldly impersonal transactions, Mary had no interest in trying to appreciate the face-to-face texture of country life, where news was passed from mouth to mouth and everyone cooperated in communal tasks like getting in the harvest. Not having to struggle for anything, I realized, also means not having to think about anything. The Crawfords, at least, were quick and clever, but Maria and Julia Bertram, praised and pampered from birth, were almost aggressively empty-headed—and their mother, of course, made of indolent stupidity a kind of art form.

I had fallen, I realized, for the oldest myth in the book: the idea that upper-class people are all urbane and cultured and intellectually sophisticated. It was probably Austen's fault as much as anyone's—all those Elizabeths and Darcys, with their crackling banter—but I only needed to look at what she herself was trying to tell us to see how ridiculous that notion was. Elegant manners and active minds are two completely different things; fat wallets and interesting thoughts have no particular connection. The upper class's traditional pursuits had a lot more to do with horses than books. As for today, those beautiful people in shining clothes don't sit around saying witty things; they drop names and talk about real estate. Matthew Arnold, who came about a half a century after Austen and who popularized the term "philistines" to describe the middle class, had an even less flattering name for the aristocracy: "barbarians." People like Elizabeth Bennet were rare exceptions. Even someone as smart as Mary Crawford preferred to exercise her body, not her brain.

But wealth and comfort, Austen made me see, stunted more than just minds. When one of the Mansfield children fell ill away from home, Fanny, who was also away, was kept informed by Lady Bertram. Yet it was as if her aunt, protected all her life from trouble or hardship or even exertion, couldn't finally feel what was going on with her own child—couldn't feel, in other words, what was going on in her own life. Her letters to Fanny, as Austen put it, were but a "medley of trusts, hopes, and fears" (as in "I trust and hope he will find the poor invalid in a less alarming state than might be apprehended"), a frictionless, conventional language that represented nothing but "a sort of playing at being frightened." Everything seemed to happen to her at one remove, as if she were handling life with gloves on.

It was just the same with the rest. With layers of money to insulate them from the consequences of their actions, nothing really mattered to them: nothing was serious, nothing was sacred, nothing could raise a genuine feeling. The idea of performance, I realized yet again, was perfectly to the point. When Henry set out to conquer Fanny's affections (a lark for him, a potential heartbreak for her), he was, in essence, mapping out a script and acting as his own director. Austen constructed those scenes—Henry reads from Shakespeare, Henry talks about giving sermons—to feel like little plays. He was playing at sensitivity, playing at cultivation, acting out whatever strategies he thought would work and savoring his performance all the while. He was impersonating himself, a spectator at his own life.

On the outing to Maria Bertram's fiancé's estate, early in the Crawfords' stay at Mansfield, the party was shown the old chapel. "Prayers were always read in it by the domestic chaplain," Maria explained, "but the late Mr. Rushworth," her fiancé's father, "left it off"—that is, discontinued the practice. "Every generation has its improvements," Mary quipped—only to eat her words a minute later, when she learned of Edmund's career plans. "'Ordained!' said Miss Crawford; 'what, are you to be a clergyman?'" She almost refused to believe it, and she certainly refused to accept it, browbeating the man she hoped to marry, over and over, to get him to change his mind. It seemed to her a kind of joke. How could anyone take religion and morality seriously? How could anyone take words like "duty" and "conduct" and "principle" seriously? After all, she never took anything seriously.

Yet as the Crawfords prolonged their stay and came to know Fanny and Edmund better and better, they began to get an inkling of everything that they'd been missing. Henry saw something in Edward that he wished he could find in himself, and something in Fanny that he wished he could have for himself. As for Mary, when she did at last tear herself away from Mansfield to pay a long-delayed visit to another friend, she had this to say to the heroine: "Mrs. Fraser has been my intimate friend for years. But I have not the least inclination to go near her. I can think only of the friends I am leaving. . . . You have all so much more *heart* among you, than one finds in the world at large." "*Heart*"—Mary's stammering attempt to name the things she was starting to learn how to value: moral serious-ness, depth of feeling, constancy of purpose. Inner riches—things you can't buy, things you have to earn. The woman who'd thought she had everything was discovering just how destitute she really was.

Yet still—and this was really the saddest thing of all, both in the novel and among the wealthy kids I knew—she couldn't finally bring herself to overcome her training. She loved Ed-mund, but she wouldn't marry him as long as he insisted on becoming a clergyman. He simply wouldn't be rich enough, though her own money was sufficient to make them both com-fortable, and he also wouldn't be glamorous enough. "For what is to be done in the church?" she asked him. "Men love to dis-tinguish themselves, and in either of the other lines," law or the military, "distinction may be gained, but not in the church. A clergyman is nothing." But of course, Mary didn't really mean that men love to distinguish themselves, though many certainly do. She meant that women love to see their men distinguished—or at least, women like her. And without dis-tinction, apparently—without success, in today's terms—a man was "nothing."

Not to be able to marry the person you love, because you love money and success more. Is there any hell worse than this? Yet I saw it all the time in New York. Even the woman I loved that summer I studied for my orals, a person of great intelli-gence and sensitivity, once admitted, with rueful self-knowledge, that she wouldn't be able to marry a man who didn't make a lot of money. She was a doctor's daughter, and had been raised in high suburban comfort. "I blame my father," she said as a sort of ironic joke. "He provided me with a certain standard of living, and now I can't do without it."

Another woman I knew, equally brilliant and self-aware but even richer and more glamorous, broke up with a man she really liked because, as she confessed, he just didn't have enough style. This was after a long string of romantic disappointments, no less. He was kind, she told me, he was attractive, he was smart, he was a good lover, he even made a very nice living. But he came from Ohio, and he didn't know how to dress or groom or distinguish himself at a cocktail party. "It's awful," she told me, "but I just can't do it."

The next time I saw her, she was being led around by a well-dressed boob who droned on about all the important people he knew. She glanced at me if to say, "I know—I'm sorry." It made me think of Maria Bertram, who also knew exactly what she was getting: "a heavy young man, with not more than common sense; but as there was nothing disagreeable in his figure or address, . . . and as a marriage with Mr. Rushworth would give her the enjoyment of a larger income than her father's," "the young lady was well pleased with her conquest." What a failure this was, of imagination as well as courage. "A large income," Mary Crawford said, "is the best recipe for happiness I ever heard of," and apparently neither she nor Maria nor many of the smart young people I knew ("It's worse than being poor!") could think of a different one.

· · ·

So was I "nothing," too? My friend and his wife once introduced me to a young couple. They seemed happy together, but,
my friend declared the moment they left, "She'll never marry
him as long as he's only a junior prosecutor." I frankly didn't
buy that for a second—I was way past taking his judgments at
face value by that point—but it gave me the final clue about his
character. *He* was the one he didn't think was good enough to
marry, good enough to love, unless he managed to make himself successful. Why else had he been so driven to fight his way
up the social ladder? Or as his wife once put it to the two of
us, consoling us for our lack of romantic cachet and looking
forward to the day when our professional accomplishments
would make us desirable to glamorous women (if there was
anyone who wanted to see her man distinguished, it was her):
"You guys are *lunch* meat now. Wait a few years—you'll be
sirloin *steak*."

Well, I didn't want to treat anyone like a piece of meat anymore, and I didn't want to be treated like one myself, not even
metaphorically. But what was the alternative? It wasn't just my
friends and their glamorous crowd. I had been learning to measure myself in terms of success—academic success, professional
success—for as long as I could remember, and everything in the
culture around me (New York was only an extreme example)
instructed me that money and status were the keys to happiness.

So I kept thinking about that word, "nothing." Who, after
all, was "nothing" if not Fanny Price—"lowest and last," as her
awful Aunt Norris reminded her. Forget Catherine Morland in

Northanger Abbey: if anyone didn't seem like she was born to be a heroine, it was Fanny. And yet that was exactly what Austen had made her. Indeed, more than Catherine or Emma or Elizabeth Bennet, she was a heroine in the oldest sense—not just a protagonist but a role model, someone we were being asked, however improbably, to emulate. Her very insignificance, I now saw, was designed to provoke us into trying to figure out what her creator found so admirable about her.

Fanny, I realized, was not just different from the privileged people around her; she was their exact opposite. They had everything and wanted more; she had little and was willing to make do with less. Instead of responding to adversity with petulance and spite, she handled it with fortitude, resilience, and, when necessary, resignation. She had hated having to leave her family and come to Mansfield when she was a little girl, but "learning to transfer in its favour much of her attachment to her former home," she "grew up there not unhappily among her cousins." "Learning" was interesting: she had to teach herself to do it, it didn't just happen by itself. "Not unhappily" was even more interesting. She wasn't happy, and given the circumstances, she didn't look like she was ever going to be, but by accepting the situation and making the best of it, she managed at least to avoid being unhappy—which was more than you could say for most of her cousins, most of the time.

Whereas Henry and the rest, always able to command amusement, were constantly dogged by the threat of boredom, Fanny had created a rich inner life for herself. The East room, her little space upstairs, was like a diorama of her mind, a place where she could always find "some pursuit, or some train of thought. . . . Her plants, her books, . . . her writing-desk, . . . her works of charity and ingenuity." She was quiet and shy, yes, but she had a lot going on beneath the surface. For that was the big surprise about her, one that it took me a very long time to see. Mary, lovely and charming, was far better able to *incite* emotions, but Fanny felt them much more keenly. She may have been prudish and prim, but she was also, of all things, intensely passionate.

Shame, gratitude, terror, happiness, jealousy, love: her emotions were not always pleasant, but she felt them with her whole body. "Fanny's feelings on the occasion were such as she believed herself incapable of expressing; but her countenance and a few artless words fully conveyed all their gratitude and delight." "He saw her lips formed into a *no,* though the sound was inarticulate, but her face was like scarlet." Life was simply much more real to her than it was to Mary or Henry or Tom or Maria. Its risks were more threatening, its pleasures more precious. One of Austen's highest lessons, I realized, is that the only people who can really feel are those who have a sense of what it means to do without.

Which was not an endorsement of poverty, either. The glimpse we got of Fanny's original family made it quite clear that Austen was not foolish enough to romanticize deprivation. The Price household was loud, chaotic, and dirty, with no more consideration for other people's feelings than prevailed at Mansfield itself. Austen's point was subtler. Being a valuable person—a "something" rather than a "nothing"—means having consideration for the people around you. Too much money renders that unnecessary; too little makes it very difficult. Fanny was a heroine, finally, because she was able to put herself aside for other people.

One of the novel's most important words was "exertion" (meaning exertion on behalf of others), and another one was "duty"—two concepts we don't hear very much about anymore, in this age of do-your-own-thing and every-man-for-himself. Fanny exerted herself for Lady Bertram and Mrs. Norris all the time—patiently, uncomplainingly—but she also coached Maria's dull-witted fiancé when he was trying to learn his lines for the play (even though she frowned upon the project) and, a far more painful sacrifice, swallowed her feelings to help Edmund rehearse his scenes with the dreaded Mary.

As for "duty," the word connected the obligations that Fanny understood herself to have as a niece, cousin, and friend with the responsibilities that Edmund looked forward to assuming as a clergyman and that William embraced as a naval officer— exactly the ideal of selfless conduct that Austen saw among the professional men in her own family (her clergyman father, her sailor brothers). The Crawfords, of course, had a different and more modern interpretation of the concept. "It is everybody's duty," Mary said, "to do as well for themselves as they can."

But the novel's most important word of all was "useful." "It is not in fine preaching only," Edmund told Mary, "that a good clergyman will be useful in his parish." Henry had sense enough to put "usefulness" next to "heroism" (the "glory" of usefulness, no less) in his admiration of William Price. Lady Bertram, not surprisingly—it was the worst thing that Austen could say about her—"never thought of being useful to anybody."

I resisted accepting this, for a long time, as a standard of behavior. It seemed so, well, utilitarian—so petty and practical. Is that the best we could do for one another, be "useful"? What about support and compassion and love? But eventually I started to see the point. Usefulness—seeing what people need and helping them get it—*is* support and compassion. Loving your friends and family is great, but what does it mean if you aren't actually willing to *do* anything for them when they really need you, put yourself out in any way? Love, I saw, is a verb, not just a noun—an effort, not just another precious feeling.

Because Fanny had to work hard, set aside her feelings, and sacrifice herself for others—to be, in a word, useful—only she possessed the moral strength to rise to the challenge when circumstances arrived—it was the climax of the novel—that put everyone to the test. As for the others (always excepting her cousin Edmund), their money had given them too much freedom. They had never had to make the kinds of tough choices that build character, and in the crunch they were, precisely, useless.

Such circumstances, Austen knew, will always eventually arrive. They came for her own family when the wife of that same wealthy brother Edward died a few days after giving birth to their eleventh child. The oldest, Fanny Knight, her favorite niece, was still only fifteen. "Edward's loss is terrible," Austen wrote her sister Cassandra, who had gone once more to Godmersham for the lying-in,

> & must be felt as such, & these are too early days indeed to think of Moderation in greif, either in him or his afflicted daughter—but soon we may hope that our dear Fanny's sense of Duty to that beloved Father will rouse her to exertion. For his sake, & as the most acceptable proof of Love to the spirit of her departed Mother, she will try to be tranquil & resigned.

What Austen recommended to us, she urged upon her nearest and dearest, too. Love means effort and self-control—for the sake of others, and thus, ultimately, for your own:

> Dearest Fanny must now look upon herself as his prime source of comfort, his dearest friend; as the Being who is gradually to supply him, to the extent that is possible, what he has lost.—This consideration will elevate & cheer her.

And so it proved to be. Writing to Cassandra a few months later—her sister was still at Godmersham, being useful herself, while Austen cared for Edward's oldest boys, who had been away at school when their mother died—she was able to say this:

> You rejoice me by what you say of Fanny. . . . We thought of & talked of her yesterday . . . & wished her a long enjoy-

ment of all the happiness to which she seems born.—While she gives happiness to those about her, she is pretty sure of her own share.

Duty, exertion, resignation, and ultimately, happiness: the same ideas that Austen would later embody in the story of that other Fanny, the one she created and sent to a place that looked a lot like Godmersham Park.

But there was one last form of usefulness (though I never would have thought of it that way) that Austen was keen to teach—so much so that she put it right up front, at the very start of the novel. The ten-year-old heroine had been at Mansfield for a week, sobbing herself to sleep every night, when her cousin Edmund, six years her senior, came upon her in tears on the attic stairs. "And sitting down by her, he was at great pains to overcome her shame, . . . and persuade her to speak openly." She missed her family, he soon perceived, and so he said, "Let us walk out in the park, and you shall tell me all about your brothers and sisters." And that was enough to win him a friend for life, the simple act of inviting Fanny to tell her story. No one else had thought to do it; no one else had thought about her at all.

How different this was, I realized, from the kinds of stories I had trained myself to tell my friend and his wife, those polished little anecdotes that had to have a laugh at every turn. "You shall tell me all about your brothers and sisters." *All* about: no impatience, no competitiveness, no interruptions, no need to worry about being entertaining, no having to watch your listeners' eyes glaze over while they thought about what they were going to say when you finally stopped talking already. Did Edmund really care about her brothers and sisters? Probably not. But he cared about her, and she cared about them, and that was enough for him. To listen to a person's stories, he understood, is to learn their feelings and experiences and values and habits of mind, and to learn them all at once and all together. Austen was not a novelist for nothing: she knew that our stories are what make us human, and that listening to someone else's stories—entering into their feelings, validating their experiences—is the highest way of acknowledging their humanity, the sweetest form of usefulness.

There's no doubt about it: fun people are fun. But I finally learned that there is something more important, in the people you know, than whether they are fun. Thinking about those friends who had given me so much pleasure but who had also caused me so much pain, thinking about that bright, cruel world to which they'd introduced me, I saw that there's a better way to value people. Not as fun or not fun, or stylish or not stylish, but as warm or cold, generous or selfish. People who think about others and people who don't. People who know how to listen, and people who only know how to talk.

I could drift away from the private-school crowd—which, now that I had gotten my head screwed on a little straighter, is exactly what I did—I could leave New York altogether, as I knew I might someday have to do, but these lessons, I real-

ized, would always apply. Few of us travel in the kinds of upper-
class circles of which I'd had a glimpse, but we all live in a
world where money and status and celebrity are cherished too
highly, and we're all susceptible to the temptation to value people for things like wealth and glamour and success—to value
ourselves for them, and sacrifice what's really important in
order to get them.

The truth is, I never did grow to like Fanny Price, and I never
could bring myself to dislike the Crawfords as much as I knew
I should. By the same token, I didn't find it easy to spend less
time with my friend and his wife. Fun is fun, and charm is
charming, and we can't really prevent ourselves from feeling
drawn to them. But the lesson of *Northanger Abbey* still applied: "Such feelings ought to be investigated, that they may
know themselves." Thinking can't stop us from feeling, but it
can stop us from acting. It can prevent us from being taken in
by our feelings.

I wasn't even sure that *Austen* expected us to like Fanny
Price. She knew quite well that Fanny would be tough to love,
but she wanted to draw the contrast with people like the Crawfords in the starkest possible terms. By not giving her heroine
any kind of wit or charm to distract us, she forced us to focus
on the things that really mattered about her. Elizabeth Bennet
also had a generous heart, was also capable of being thoughtful
and selfless, but with her glorious lovability, who even bothered
to notice? Reading about her, it was all too easy to imagine that
Austen only cared about sparkle and wit.

That was why she had to make her heroine in *Mansfield
Park* so dull. This time, she took Elizabeth and split her person-

ality in half: Mary got the charm, Fanny got the goodness, and we had to decide which one was better. Austen wasn't really condemning brightness and energy, I realized; she was just showing us that they aren't the most important things in life. "Wisdom is better than Wit," she wrote to Fanny Knight the very year that *Mansfield Park* was published, "& in the long run will certainly have the laugh on her side." Choosing Fanny-ness over Mary-ness does not come naturally and is not always particularly pleasant, but, Austen was telling us, it is what we need to do.

And so, it is what I began to try to do. I knew perfectly well that I fell far short of the standards that Austen was holding up, so I started to watch myself, and I started, yes, to exert myself. I made a deliberate effort to be useful to the people around me, whether it was something small, like showing up on time for dinner, or something bigger, like proofreading a friend's dissertation. Most of all, I practiced sitting still and listening—really listening. To friends, to students, even just to people I met, as their stories came stumbling out in the awkward, unpolished way that people have when you give them the freedom to speak from the heart. People's stories are the most personal thing they have, and paying attention to those stories is just about the most important thing you can do for them. I never did come to like Fanny's story, but that's the deepest lesson that finally listening to it had taught me.

CHAPTER 5

persuasion
true friends

Meanwhile, as I stumbled in and out of the social elite, I spent the bulk of my time slaving away at, procrastinating on, whimpering about, and otherwise slogging through my dissertation. There's nothing quite like writing a dissertation. You've gone through almost twenty years of school, including your first few years as a graduate student, and you've always had someone there to tell you what to do: take these courses, do this reading, answer these questions. You've also always had other people around to share the experience with—sit next to in class, bitch to about your teachers, study with for exams.

Then, all of a sudden, you're on your own. It's like being left in the woods without a map. Good luck, sucker. Drop us a line if you make it out alive. All you know is that you have to go off by yourself for four or five or six years and write what amounts to a book. You've never written a book, you have no idea how to write one, and no one, you quickly realize, is going to teach you, because the only way to learn is just to do it. Plus, you have to make up your own topic. And, oh yes, it has to be completely original.

I had decided to write my dissertation about community in nineteenth-century English fiction. The Austen chapter would be followed by ones on George Eliot (yes, the once-dreaded *Middlemarch*) and Joseph Conrad (my old standby). It was a very personal decision. The most important experience of my life had been the years I had spent in a Jewish youth movement during high school. For most people, that kind of thing is an eye-rolling waste of time—a nerd festival that your parents force you into when you'd rather be out behind the mall, smoking cigarettes and trying to get to second base.

But this was different, at least for my friends and me. We ran the thing on our own, more or less—even the "adults," who had gone through the movement themselves, were mainly in their early twenties—and it was about discovering our own values and developing our own sense of authenticity. It was a national movement, too, with chapters and regions and camps, and kids who came from exotic places like Oregon and Illinois. It was, to the extent that we could manage it, a complete world, or at least, a complete worldview, and we were there because it gave us all the things we couldn't find in the high-school jungle: a feeling of acceptance, an outlet for idealism, a sense of being part of something bigger than ourselves.

In a word—and it was a word that we used all the time— community. The dream we all had was to move to Israel and live on a kibbutz, a sort of Jewish version of a commune. It was a dream about sharing everything and being together forever. But however naïve the idea might have been, it meant that while we were dreaming about community, we were also living it. We would come together, in our dozens or our hundreds, for meetings and weekends and trips and summers; for songs, games, campfires, and an endless string of nights when we just stayed up and talked.

We talked about social justice and social action, idealism and identity, being Jewish and being human. We talked, until we could barely keep our eyes open, just to have an excuse to stay up together, just to feel each other nearby. We were going to change the world, but along the way, without even noticing it, we changed ourselves. It was the place where I made my closest friends, found my voice, and learned to think about the world. Where I kissed my first girl one summer and lost my virginity a couple of summers after that. Where I felt more at home than I did in my actual home.

We were escaping from high school, but it was not lost on us, even then, that a lot of us were also escaping from our families. That's a natural thing to want to do when you're a teenager, but I, like many of my friends, had a good deal of extra incentive.

Things were not good at home, and they never had been. The same emotional violence that my father inflicted on us, he also inflicted on my mother. I'm not sure which was worse for me. With me and her, it had always been the most primitive, unspoken kind of monkey love—the deep comfort, even as a teenager, of just being around her. We'd hang out in the kitchen sometimes after school, and I would listen to her stories, which were all about the happy life she'd lived growing up in Toronto, before she met my father. (She, too, had been in a Jewish youth movement, and she totally understood why it meant so much to me. My father was more ambivalent. He liked that it kept me affiliated, so long as I didn't take that kibbutz stuff too seriously.) Even then I sensed that somehow, by listening, I was making it up to her for my father's rage and ridicule, just as she had always tried to shield and solace me. We were secret allies with a common foe, even if we couldn't come right out and say it.

But then my father would explode into the house, and all bets were off. He was really quite inventive when it came to finding ways of tormenting her. A memory from early childhood: My mother comes into the living room to announce that supper's ready—the supper she's been working on the whole afternoon. My father ignores her and keeps on reading the paper. He'll be damned if he's going to give her the satisfaction. Something like half an hour later, so much later that my mother's announcement has started to feel like a dream—he couldn't have just ignored her, right?—I realize how hungry I am and dare to ask, "Didn't Mommy say that supper was ready a long time ago?"

Such was the level of emotional discourse, and that was a relatively placid evening, because they hadn't been screaming at each other from the moment he'd come home. A lot of days were like a running battle, a knife fight with words. Years later, I was bickering with a girlfriend one night before dinner. As I sat down to eat with a gut so clenched that I could barely choke back the food, I was hit by a wave of nostalgia. *Yes,* I thought, *I know this feeling. This is what my childhood felt like.*

Was it any wonder that I clung to the movement like a cat on a tree? We clung to each other, my friends and I; we were all, in some way, in flight.

But youth movement ended, because youth does. Like a lot of my friends, I became one of those "adults" myself in college—a counselor, a leader. But eventually we all just, so to speak, ran out of movement to be part of. We had no choice but to go our separate ways, and I was left wandering the world to mourn that titanic experience, wondering how I was ever going to find something like it again. By the time I moved to Brooklyn, seven years later, I was going in the opposite direction fast, into the solitude of my apartment and the loneliness of my work. College itself was long gone, my grad-school classmates were tunneling into their own dissertations, and what friends I still had, from the movement or elsewhere, had scattered themselves across the country.

One was in Boston, doing a postdoc; one was in Chicago, studying religion; one was in Kansas, becoming a mom; one was in California, working in film. My very closest friend, the one who knew me better than I knew myself—she was also just about my last remaining link to the movement—had settled in New Hampshire and was starting her own design business. They were all living their separate lives, and the older we grew, the worse it got. The prospect of recapturing that sense of community, that feeling of belonging to something, seemed more remote than ever. So when I had to choose a topic for my dissertation, I decided to study what I couldn't experience. It was a classic academic move. Since I didn't have community, I would spend my time thinking about it.

Two years into Brooklyn, I was still working on my Austen chapter. The thing was like a chronic illness, my only comfort being the grad-school adage that once you've finished your first chapter, you're halfway through the dissertation, because writing the first one teaches you how to write the rest.

I had chosen to begin with Austen not only because I loved her work so much, but also because she seemed to me to represent the perfect starting point for my investigation: a writer who had celebrated community in its most basic and traditional sense—the settled, stable rural world, that good green place where everybody knows you and everybody belongs, the exact image of what I was trying to recapture in my own life. I had also decided to focus on my two favorite among her novels—*Pride and Prejudice*, of course, and the book that had long since won a special place in my heart, and now increasingly reflected my state of mind, *Persuasion*.

Austen's final work, *Persuasion* was unique among her novels for its layered emotional texture and profound depth of feeling. The mood was wistful, melancholy, autumnal, projecting an atmosphere of nostalgia and regret that was unlike anything she had created before. A work of loneliness and loss, the novel was completed less than a year before Austen's death. Whether she knew that she was dying by then—the illness that came upon her in the middle of writing the book was mysterious and, for a long time, intermittent—it was impossible to say.

What seemed clearer—Austen turned forty during the novel's composition—was that *Persuasion* reflected the ripened outlook of a woman who felt herself to be passing into the next phase of life.

The novel's special place among her work was clear from its very first chapter. The heroine, Anne Elliot, was not a blooming girl of seventeen or twenty, a Catherine Morland or Elizabeth Bennet springing lightly over the threshold of adulthood and into the adventure of romance; she was already twenty-seven, still young by our standards but well past her prime by those of Austen's day. Anne had already had her novel, so to speak, and it had ended in failure. Eight years earlier, she had fallen rapidly and deeply in love with a dashing young naval officer named Captain Wentworth. Wentworth was modeled on Austen's brother Frank. Both made captain at a young age; both fought in the great Battle of San Domingo. Even their first names were similar: Wentworth's was Frederick. Both also came ashore after that momentous engagement to get themselves a wife, but while Frank did marry his bride in that summer of 1806, Anne and Wentworth's romance only led to grief.

He was "a remarkably fine young man, with a great deal of intelligence, spirit, and brilliancy." She was "an extremely pretty girl, with gentleness, modesty, taste, and feeling." But she also came from a family of aristocratic snobs that made the Bertrams of *Mansfield Park* look like socialists. A young man without wealth or pedigree was just not going to do. Anne's father, the odious Sir Walter—spiteful, shallow, and vain—"thought it a very degrading alliance" and "gave it all the negative of great astonishment, great coldness, great silence, and a professed resolution of doing nothing for his daughter" (that is, refusing to give her a dowry). Anne's mother, Lady Elliot, a warm and decent woman whose excellent judgment had saved her husband from the worst consequences of his character, might have seen to it that justice was done after all, but she had died when Anne was fourteen, and her place in Anne's life had been taken by Lady Elliot's best friend, Lady Russell.

Lady Russell appreciated the heroine as her father never did—Anne's virtues were far too fine for Sir Walter to know how to value them—but she was no more cheerful about the match. "Anne Elliot, with all her claims of birth, beauty, and mind, to throw herself away at nineteen! . . . Anne Elliot, so young; known to so few, to be snatched off by a stranger without alliance or fortune!" It was the same snobbery with a kinder face. And so, without a friend to take her side, Anne was pressured into breaking the engagement. Wentworth went off in anger and resentment, and Anne, her bloom ruined and her spirits sunk, was left to waste her youth in the bitterness of futile regret.

Flash forward eight years, and the heroine was more alone than ever now, alone in a way that none of Austen's other characters were. Even Fanny Price, in *Mansfield Park,* had her cousin Edmund and her brother William and the genuine if lazy affection of her aunt Lady Bertram. But while Anne still had Lady Russell, for what she was worth, that was all she had. Having never gotten over Captain Wentworth, she had refused the hand of a local gentleman a few years later, and she seemed to have no chance of ever being offered someone else's. Her younger sister, Mary, had gotten married herself (to Charles Musgrove, the same local man whom Anne refused). Her older sister, Elizabeth, was as cold and mean as their father—one of the things that made her Sir Walter's favorite—and equally awful to Anne. Isolated in her own family, the heroine "was nobody with either father or sister; her word had no weight, her convenience was always to give way: she was only Anne."

Fanny also had Mansfield Park to hold on to, but now Anne was even going to lose her own beloved home. Sir Walter, with a very high opinion as to what so great a man deserved, had run himself into such a morass of debt that he was forced to rent out the family manor and move to Bath. Elizabeth would be coming along, of course, but her chosen companion would be, not the sister whose excellence she could never perceive, but an oily young widow named Mrs. Clay, all flattery and compliance, who had worked her way into Elizabeth's affections.

Anne would go to stay with the Musgroves and play the role of spinster aunt that Austen knew herself by then so very well. She would take care of her nephews while Mary, a world-class whiner, complained about how put-upon she was; she would play dances for Charles's lively, lovely younger sisters Henrietta and Louisa (who resembled Austen heroines far more than Anne now did); she would listen to everybody's grievances about one another; she would make peace between them when she could; and above all, she would stay in the shadows, where a spinster belonged. It was to be a lesson, she mused, "in the art of knowing our own nothingness beyond our own circle"— not that Anne was much of anything even *in* her own circle.

. . .

My circumstances, needless to say, were very different from Anne's, but I shared her feelings of loneliness and melancholy. I hadn't lost a parent or a home, but I had done what I could—what I had to do—to distance myself from both. I had wanted to be on my own, and now I was. I just didn't realize quite how on my own I was going to be. When you're young—when you're in high school and college and even your early twenties—you take your friends for granted. Of course they'll always be there. You take *friends* for granted. Why would you ever have trouble making new ones? Then all of a sudden—and it can feel very sudden indeed—everybody's gone. Some have moved, some have married, everyone's busy, and the crowd of potential friends by which you've always been surrounded has evaporated.

I still didn't want to get married, but I didn't want to be alone, either. Yet just as it was for Anne, that's how it was starting to look like it was always going to be for me. I still loved living in my own place and being out from under my father's shadow, but my Austen chapter wasn't taking me forever just because it gave me so much work to do. A lot of days, I didn't even have the strength to face it. I would drag myself out of bed, only to sit around and stare off into space. The air would sag, the clock would point its contemptuous hands, my cat would look at me and seem to wonder why I wasn't moving. I would feel ugly and worthless. Anne was depressed—that's what it meant for Austen to say that her spirits were low—and let's face it, so was I.

Austen herself had lost a home, a circumstance that Anne's

experience undoubtedly reflected. Right around her twenty-fifth birthday, Austen's parents suddenly announced that her father would be retiring—he had been rector of the same parish for forty years—and that they and the girls, Cassandra and Jane, would be picking up and moving, just like Sir Walter, to Bath. The news came as a terrible shock, and there was little time to get used to it. Within a couple of months, the household in which Austen had lived her entire life was going to be broken up.

Friends would have to be taken leave of, a world of familiar feelings left behind. Most of the family's things were not even transferred to Bath, but sold or given away to Austen's brother James and his wife, Anna, who were coming to take possession of the house: the piano on which Austen had learned to play; the family pictures and furniture, companions of many years; her father's library—"my books," as she called them—whose value to her we can only imagine. Austen was even pressured into surrendering one of her own important possessions, a move she defied with tart indignation. "As I do not choose to have Generosity dictated to me," she wrote to Cassandra, "I shall not resolve on giving my Cabinet to Anna till the first thought of it has been my own." From a life of rural rhythms and settled routines, she was being hustled out of the only home she'd ever known.

Four years later, years of upheaval and adjustment, came another blow that would echo through Anne's story: Austen's beloved father died. "The loss of such a Parent must be felt," she wrote to Frank, "or we should be Brutes." "His tenderness as a Father, who can do justice to?" Austen's mother was no Sir

Walter, but she was a difficult, hypochondriacal woman whom Austen poked fun at to Cassandra, and there seems little doubt that her father was the author's favorite, just as Anne's mother was hers.

After the Reverend Austen's death, four more years of uncertainty followed before Austen's mother and the girls would find a permanent home. The young woman who had tossed off three novels before the age of twenty-four—early drafts of *Pride and Prejudice, Sense and Sensibility,* and *Northanger Abbey*—was virtually silent, artistically speaking, during this entire eight-year stretch. The one piece of work that survives, the beginning of a novel called *The Watsons,* was abandoned after a few dozen pages. Was Austen discouraged at the fate of her previous work? (*Pride and Prejudice* was rejected sight unseen; *Northanger Abbey* was bought for ten pounds but never published.) Did she need stability to do her work?

Both undoubtedly were true, but Anne's story makes us suspect that the formerly ebullient young writer was also suffering from her own feelings of depression. *The Watsons,* about a group of poor, unmarried sisters trying to figure out how to save themselves from destitution before the death of their ailing clergyman father—and thus a frighteningly close parallel to Jane and Cassandra's situation—has been called "grim," "bleak," and "pessimistic." Austen, said one critic, "seems to be struggling with a peculiar oppression, a stiffness and heaviness that threatens her style." And that was *before* her father died—an event itself preceded, by only a couple of months, by the death of Anne Lefroy, the surrogate mother who had been a crucial figure in Austen's life since childhood. No wonder she couldn't summon the will to write.

One more circumstance must have contributed to Austen's portrait of Anne, as well as to the novel's somber atmosphere as a whole. At around the age of twenty-seven, the same age as the heroine, Austen rejected what she must have known would be her last chance at marriage. The man in question was Harris Bigg-Wither, brother to a trio of old friends and heir to a large estate, but a shy and awkward young man who was five years Austen's junior. She accepted his proposal one evening, agonized about it the entire night, then rescinded her acceptance the next morning. It was, she surely knew, a decisive step. From there, says Austen biographer Claire Tomalin, she "hurried into middle age," embracing the role of maiden aunt for once and for all. She was not lonely, but in a profound sense, she would always be alone. Now, in Anne, she created a heroine who was staring over the same cliff.

It was no accident that the novel began in autumn, or that Anne dwelled, like none of Austen's other heroines, in the past and her own mind. On a walk with Henrietta and Louisa Musgrove and some of the other young people, while the rest of them chattered away, Anne mused wistfully on the declining year. Austen's language swelled with unaccustomed feeling here, its normally satirical accents drawn, almost against their will, into a slower, more pensive rhythm. Anne's own pleasure in the walk, we learned,

must arise from the exercise and the day, from the view of
the last smiles of the year upon the tawny leaves and with-
ered hedges, and from repeating to herself some few of the
thousand poetical descriptions extant of autumn,—that
season of peculiar and inexhaustible influence on the mind
of taste and tenderness,—that season which had drawn
from every poet, worthy of being read, some attempt at de-
scription, or some lines of feeling.

And when something happened to interrupt her train of
thought, a reminder of her own exclusion from the dance of
youth, "the sweet scenes of autumn were for a while put by,
unless some tender sonnet, fraught with the apt analogy of the
declining year, with declining happiness, and the images of
youth and hope, and spring, all gone together, blessed her
memory."

But by then her memory had had a very different kind of
work to do. When Sir Walter had decamped for Bath, he had
rented the Elliot manor to a navy man, Admiral Croft, whose
wife turned out to be none other than the sister of a certain
Captain Wentworth—the very man the heroine had loved and
lost those eight long years before. "A few months more," said
Anne when she had heard the news, "and *he*, perhaps, may be
walking here."

And so indeed it proved to be. And when the dreaded meeting came,

a thousand feelings rushed on Anne, of which this was the
most consoling, that it would soon be over. . . . Her eye

half met Captain Wentworth's, a bow, a curtsey passed; she heard his voice; . . . the room seemed full, full of persons and voices, but a few minutes ended it. . . . The room was cleared, and Anne might finish her breakfast as she could.

"It is over! it is over!" she repeated to herself again and again, in nervous gratitude. "The worst is over!"

Mary talked, but she could not attend. She had seen him. They had met. They had been once more in the same room.

Soon, however, she began to reason with herself, and try to be feeling less. . . .

Alas! with all her reasoning, she found, that to retentive feelings eight years may be little more than nothing.

But if the past was instantly revived for Anne, the case was very different for her former fiancé. "Henrietta asked him what he thought of you," reported Mary in her passive-aggressive way, "and he said, 'You were so altered he should not have known you again.'"

Yet painful as the meeting was, Wentworth's arrival began to draw Anne away from her awful family and toward a very different group of people. Wentworth's fellow officer and close friend, Captain Harville, was now living with his wife in the nearby seaside town of Lyme. When the whole group decided to pay them a visit—Henrietta and Louisa, Charles and Mary, Wentworth and Anne—the heroine discovered a kind of togetherness that she had never suspected.

Captain Harville's sister had been engaged to a third officer, Captain Benwick, but she had died before the couple could be married. And yet, Anne learned, "The friendship between him and the Harvilles seemed, if possible, augmented by the event which closed all their views of alliance, and Captain Benwick was now living with them entirely." It was the same note, and the same word—"friendship"—that marked every description of this group of naval companions. When Wentworth had complained to his sister, Admiral Croft's wife, that women are too delicate to have aboard a ship—she herself having passed many a voyage aboard her husband's—she pointed out that Wentworth had once transported Captain Harville's wife and children himself. "Where was this superfine, extraordinary sort of gallantry of yours then?" she teased. "All merged in my friendship," Wentworth replied. "I would assist any brother officer's wife that I could, and I would bring anything of Harville's from the world's end, if he wanted it."

Again, when the Harvilles met the visitors in Lyme, "nothing could be more pleasant than their desire of considering the whole party as friends of their own, because the friends of Captain Wentworth, or more kindly hospitable than their entreaties for their all promising to dine with them." And when "they all went in-doors with their new friends," the visitors "found rooms so small as none but those who invite from the heart could think capable of accommodating so many." "Friendship," "friendship," "friends," "friends": the point was not lost on the heroine, but the more she was pleased by what she saw— the more the captains and Mrs. Harville revealed their mutual warmth and generosity and goodwill—the more she was pained. "'These would have been all my friends,' was her thought; and she had to struggle against a great tendency to lowness."

＊   ＊   ＊

Anne found, at Lyme, what she did not know that she'd been searching for: something to belong to. And as I thought about the novel more deeply than I ever had before, thought about what it was saying about the ways that people attach themselves to one another, the ways that they belong together, I realized that this, and nothing else, was Austen's image of community—this group of friends.

I had been looking in the wrong place, both in her novels and in my own life. I had come to Austen imagining that I would find a picture of that idyllic rural community that we all carry around in our heads. And I had dimly supposed that if I was ever going to find another community myself, it was going to have to resemble something like that. Now I saw that community, in the modern world, would never be a structure you could put your hands on—something regular or stable or permanent. It would not resemble a kibbutz or a commune, both of which made that exact mistake of trying to turn back the clock to an earlier state of existence. Nor would it resemble a youth movement, which, like the other communities that young people pass through (and which, like me, they often later pine for)—a high school or a college, a sports team or fraternity or summer camp—is the kind of all-encompassing environment that can only exist when you're young. The modern world, I began to understand, was far too unstable for anything like that, modern relationships too fluid. For adults today, it seemed to me now, community can only be a circle of friends.

Still, that was relatively easy for me to see, two centuries into the modern age and with the help of Austen. The wonder was how she had managed to see it herself, at a time when modernity was still just getting off the ground, and from her little perch in rural England. Because what *Persuasion* dramatized, I now saw, was nothing less than the passing of the traditional world. The community that Austen was rejecting—or at least, bidding farewell—was rural England itself: the very thing I had come to her to find. Rejecting its hierarchy, the feudal order that the smug and pompous Sir Walter, like the odious Bertrams of *Mansfield Park,* embodied. Bidding farewell to its sense of rootedness and intimacy and continuity—which she had indeed celebrated, but only once, I now saw, only in *Emma,* her one truly idyllic work.

Now, the strange thing was that *Emma* was written immediately before *Persuasion.* Only four months separated the end of work on one novel and the beginning of work on the next. But Austen could think extremely fast. From her picture of a timeless England she moved in one step to a picture of England in the middle of head-spinning change. *Emma,* which contained no dates, seemed to occur outside of history. *Persuasion,* which began with a flurry of dates, was set at a very precise historical moment: the end of the Napoleonic Wars. Austen saw, with amazing clairvoyance, that the world she had always known was about to start to disappear. The old order was yielding, however slowly, to the new. Sir Walter was packing his bags and moving aside for Admiral Croft. Aristocracy was giving way to meritocracy, hierarchy to equality. People would henceforth be bound, more and more, not as master and servant or landlord and tenant (or even as husband and wife, in the traditional, unequal fashion) but rather as friend and friend.

Yet the traditional system that put a Sir Walter above a Captain Wentworth was not the only thing, I saw, that Austen turned away from in *Persuasion*. As hard as it was to believe, she seemed to turn away from family itself. By gravitating toward the men and women of the navy, Anne was hoping that she wouldn't have to spend the rest of her life putting up with her miserable father and sisters. In fact, she avoided her family more and more as the novel went on. After the trip to Lyme, the day finally came for her to join Sir Walter and Elizabeth in Bath—not that anybody really wanted it, but she couldn't stay with her sister Mary forever—yet she tried, when she got there, to spend as little time with them as she could. Instead, she immersed herself in the company of her new friends from the navy, who had come to Bath on holiday, as well.

Indeed, Anne's disaffection with her family achieved remarkable heights. Late in the novel, she got wind of an intrigue that severely threatened her father and sister's peace. Ordinarily that sort of development would have moved to the center of the plot, with the heroine hastening to spread the news and avert disaster. Here she never even got around to passing it along. Her family simply didn't matter to her anymore.

How could this be, I wondered. How could Austen, the great novelist of romance, the great maker of marriages, be against family? Yet when I thought back to her other books, I realized that there was scarcely a happy family among them—ten unhappy ones, by my count, and no more than one of the other kind (and that was only Emma and her father, as much a kind of marriage as a family). And while she always got her heroines married, she never followed their stories beyond the bliss of couplehood and into the complications that followed, the battle of children and parents. Her own family, by all accounts, was happy, and she clearly enjoyed her nieces and nephews, but when she imagined felicity, she always drew a picture of a bond among adults—couples and friends and the little circles, the miniature communities, they make together.

For once I saw this pattern in *Persuasion,* I looked and found it everywhere. Yes, Austen made sure to find her heroines a husband, but she also took care to build them a community— a sphere of husbands and wives and brothers and sisters to live their marriages within. *Pride and Prejudice* ended, not with one wedding but with two, a pair of sisters marrying a pair of friends and gathering additional siblings to them. *Emma* ended with three, and the heroine's, we were told, was sped along by "the wishes, the hopes, the confidence, the predictions of the small band of true friends who witnessed the ceremony." It was no surprise that one critic called friendship, for Austen, "the true light of life."

Friends, Austen taught me, are the family you choose. But while the notion has become a commonplace of late, Austen, I realized, saw a step further. We make our friends our family, but we also make our family—or some of them—our friends.

William Price, in *Mansfield Park,* was Fanny's "brother and friend." Catherine Morland, in *Northanger Abbey,* made friends with Henry and Eleanor Tilney, who were friends with each other but not with their treacherous older brother. Elizabeth Bennet was friends with Jane and her father but couldn't stand her mother or her other sisters; the community that formed at the end of *Pride and Prejudice* included some relatives but pointedly excluded others.

Anne herself, Austen told us, found no reason to be jealous of Henrietta and Louisa Musgrove, her sister Mary's sisters-in-law—pleasant, pretty girls who didn't have a whole lot going on upstairs—except for this one thing: "that seemingly perfect good understanding and agreement together, that good-humoured mutual affection, of which she had known so little herself with either of her sisters." The Harvilles, one of the few happy families in Austen's work, included a friend, Captain Benwick, as part of their household; the circle of nautical friends included a brother and sister, Captain Wentworth and Mrs. Croft. Friendship and family can blur together, Austen was showing me—the groups intersecting, the feelings intermingling.

No one understood this more intimately than Austen herself. Everywhere in her letters, the terms and accents of family and friendship intertwine. What was her impulse to accept the hand of Harris Bigg-Wither, misguided though she soon realized it to be, if not a desire to create a family with his sisters, her friends? Her own sister, Cassandra, of course, was her very best, her lifelong friend, but her favorite niece won entrance to the circle at the early age of fifteen. "I am greatly pleased with your account of Fanny," Jane wrote Cassandra. "I found her in the summer just what you describe, almost another Sister, & could not have supposed that a niece would ever have been so much to me."

Later, with Fanny in her twenties, niece and aunt exchanged letters of exquisite intimacy, in one of which the older woman exclaimed, "You can hardly think what a pleasure it is to me, to have such thorough pictures of your Heart." But, she added, fearing that the circle would someday be broken, "Oh! what a loss it will be, when you are married." Cassandra surely knew that she was speaking for both survivors when, in the wake of Austen's death, she wrote her niece—"doubly dear to me now for her dear sake whom we have lost"—"I *have* lost a treasure, such a Sister, such a friend as never can be surpassed."

Jane and Cassandra's household, the one they shared with their mother for the last twelve years of Austen's life, was itself a little community of family and friends, just like the Harvilles'. The role of Captain Benwick was assumed by Martha Lloyd, a childhood friend who grew closer to Austen than anyone but her sister. The two had laughed together in bed when Austen was a teenager, and Martha moved in with the Austen women the year that both Jane's father and Martha's widowed mother died—an arrangement that was not uncommon at the time. She stayed there until her marriage to Austen's brother Frank—being dragged by Jane to the theater, listening to the author's views on politics, royal scandal, and her own career,

and generally being, as Jane told Cassandra, "the friend &
Sister under every circumstance."

Friends may be the family you choose, but I was still no closer
to being part of such a circle than Anne had been at Lyme. In
fact, I was having as much difficulty as she did simply finding
individual friends, let alone a whole circle of them. The terrain
had shifted when I wasn't looking. People were not just busier
than they used to be, they also weren't as open. That youthful
flexibility, that eagerness for new experiences and new people,
that Austen celebrated in *Northanger Abbey*—it seemed to be
draining away as we rounded the corner and headed into our
thirties. You could no longer just meet someone and dive right
into a friendship, as you'd been able to when you were fifteen
or twenty or even twenty-five. The people I met now, potential
friends, seemed cagier, less trusting, more defended. Making a
friend had become a whole project, like a high-level diplomatic
negotiation or a complicated puzzle that you could only fill in
a couple of pieces at a time.

Austen herself cared far too much about friendship to make
the mistake of idealizing it. She knew all about what Fanny
Price, in *Mansfield Park,* referred to as "the different sorts of
friendship in the world," and she had written about them from
the time she was a girl. In her teenage years, the fashion had been
for what they called romantic friendships—histrionically passionate attachments designed to show off your susceptibility to
fine emotion. *Love and Freindship*, the most famous of her
adolescent satires ("as fast as she could write and quicker than

she could spell," as Virginia Woolf remarked about them), was designed to deflate that exact cliché:

> *After having been deprived during the course of 3 weeks of a real freind, . . . imagine my transports at beholding one, most truly worthy of the Name. . . . She was all sensibility and Feeling. We flew into each other's arms and after having exchanged vows of mutual Freindship for the rest of our Lives, instantly unfolded to each other the most inward secrets of our Hearts.*

One can only imagine the fun that Austen would have made of Facebook or MySpace or Twitter, with their comparable illusion of instantaneous intimacy. Isabella Thorpe tried to pull the same kind of thing with Catherine Morland in *Northanger Abbey*, but in her later books, Austen moved on to more adult forms of insincerity. Social climbers, she knew, can exercise their limbs on friendship as well as marriage, and the world of *Persuasion* was crawling with them. The town of Bath was a full immersion in the tepid waters of social ambition. Mrs. Clay, the oily widow, had hooked herself onto Elizabeth Elliot to see how far the ride would take her, her ultimate purpose being to inveigle Sir Walter into making her his second wife— at which point, we could be sure, the new Lady Elliot would no longer bother being deferential to her "friend." "Frenemy," we sometimes call this sort of person now, the kind who's nice just long enough to get whatever they think they can out of you.

The novel's most avid lickspittle, however, turned out to be none other than Sir Walter himself. This made perfect sense once I thought about it. Anyone that invested in distinctions of social rank had to be as obsequious to those above him as he was contemptuous of those below. Just as bullies are cowards in disguise, snobs are secret grovelers—another reason Austen so adored the aristocracy. The object of Sir Walter's particular veneration was a cousin, the Viscountess Dalrymple, and her daughter, Miss Carteret, a pair of mediocrities who turned out to have nothing going for them but their pedigree:

> *Anne had never seen her father and sister before in contact with nobility, and she must acknowledge herself disappointed. She had hoped better things from their high ideas of their own situation in life, and was reduced to form a wish which she had never foreseen,—a wish that they had more pride; for "our cousins Lady Dalrymple and Miss Carteret," "our cousins, the Dalrymples," sounded in her ears all day long.*

But the friendship of a Sir Walter or a Mrs. Clay was not likely to take in anyone less susceptible to flattery than their intended targets. Far more dangerous, Austen wanted us to know—and far more insidious—were the friends who actually did mean well but couldn't tell the difference between what was good for you and what was only good for them. Such a friend was Lady Russell, and the saddest thing about Anne's relationship with her, her surrogate mother and only intimate, was just how much the heroine actually valued her, how little she could afford to let herself see the older woman's limitations. Anne thought, early on, "of the extraordinary blessing of having one such truly sympathising friend as Lady Russell," but only after the perfectly blasé reception she received at the Musgroves' (that lesson "in the art of knowing our own nothingness beyond our own circle"). Even her sister Mary had treated the whole trauma of surrendering the family estate, which Anne had been suffering through for weeks, as a matter of utter indifference. Anyone was going to look good compared to that.

Yet it was that same Lady Russell who had pressured the heroine into making the worst mistake of her life, rejecting Captain Wentworth. Of course, she did it for what she thought were all the right reasons. Still, late in the novel, when she was presented with the same kind of situation again, she gave, unbelievably, the same advice—even though she knew perfectly well how terribly alone Anne was and how miserable she had been for all those years. But even Anne, by then, could see the truth. Lady Russell, whether she recognized it or not, was trying to protect her own dignity, not her friend's. *She* was the person she was trying to save from being connected with someone as lowly as a naval officer.

This was a woman, after all, who thought that kissing up to the Viscountess Dalrymple sounded like a really good idea. Indeed, once the heroine took a hard look at her friend, she figured out that there wasn't a whole lot of difference, in their ideas about class and manners and what really mattered in a person, between Lady Russell and her own father. And so, once Anne had made up her mind about how she was going to live her life—uninfluenced, this time, by any of her "friends"—

"there was nothing less for Lady Russell to do," if she wanted to stay on good terms with the heroine, "than to admit that she had been pretty completely wrong, and to take up a new set of opinions." In plain language, Anne told Lady Russell to go soak her head. The heroine had walked away from her father and sisters, and she was strong enough now to do the same to anyone else who stood in the way of her happiness.

I saw this kind of thing all the time back then—friends who thought they were looking after your happiness when they were really just trying to protect their own. People pressuring you to break up with someone they didn't like, or stay together with someone they did. People wanting you to get married already, like they had, or stay single, because they didn't want to be the last ones left alone. I'm sure I did that sort of thing myself. There's nothing deliberate about it, as Austen knew; it just takes a lot of self-awareness, as well as a lot of generosity, to remove your own desires from the equation.

The couple who introduced me to the private-school crowd, needless to say, did not possess a great deal of either. "Thank God that's over!" they said when I told them about a certain new relationship—"that" being my long string of romantic failures, the source of all those funny stories I used to entertain them with. However kindly it was meant, the statement came to exert an unmistakable pressure, as the months went by and the relationship soured, to stay coupled up. "That" was supposed to be over; I couldn't disappoint them by going back to "that." And when I did finally break off the relationship, their response, while undoubtedly well intentioned, was not exactly consoling.

"We're just sorry that there won't ever be any little Billys run-ning around." Wait—ever? You mean you're closing the books on me? It sure sounded like they were—like I had proved to them, for once and for all, just how completely hopeless I was.

True friendship, like true love, was pretty rare in Austen's view. "Here and there, human nature may be great in times of trial," said a character in *Persuasion,* "but generally speaking . . . it is selfishness and impatience rather than generosity and forti-tude, that one hears of. There is so little real friendship in the world!" The person who made that statement, a Mrs. Smith, had had a difficult life. She had traveled, Anne reflected, "among that part of mankind which made her think worse of the world than she hoped it deserved"—that is, than Anne hoped it de-served. But that was all that she could do—hope. She knew that Mrs. Smith, who "had lived very much in the world," had seen a great deal more of life than had the sheltered heroine herself. And after all, her new acquaintance with the people of the navy notwithstanding, her own experience offered precious little with which to dispute the other woman's views.

Yet Anne's relationship with Mrs. Smith turned out to be one of those rare, true friendships itself. The two had known each other at the boarding school where Anne was sent in the wake of her mother's death, "grieving for the loss of a mother whom she had dearly loved, feeling her separation from home, and suffer-ing as a girl of fourteen, of strong sensibility and not high spir-its, must suffer at such a time." The future Mrs. Smith, three years older, "had shewn her kindness, . . . had been useful and good to her in a way which had considerably lessened her misery." Usefulness and kindness—those same standards of human decency that Austen had championed in *Mansfield Park*, and that mattered to her more than all the wit in the world.

Now it was the turn of Mrs. Smith to need some kindness. Having lost her husband, her money, and even the use of her legs, she was living, when Anne rediscovered her, in a couple of dark, comfortless rooms with scarcely a soul even to help her get from one to the other. Sir Walter couldn't believe his ears when he got wind of the fact that his daughter had taken to seeing such a person. "'Westgate Buildings!' said he; 'and who is Miss Anne Elliot to be visiting in Westgate Buildings? A Mrs. Smith. A widow Mrs. Smith. . . . And what is her attraction? That she is old and sickly. Upon my word, Miss Anne Elliot, you have the most extraordinary taste!'"

But the truest act of friendship belonged, in the end, to Mrs. Smith herself. She knew something, it turned out: something about someone very close to Anne, something that all the rules of propriety—and far more important, something that her own dire self-interest—dictated that she not reveal. Yet Anne's own welfare did dictate that she reveal it. Mrs. Smith was no saint. She struggled with what to do. She had very few hopes of improving her wretched situation in life, and by revealing what she knew, she would destroy the newest and the best of them. It would have been far better for her if she had simply kept her mouth shut. But she took a deep breath, and she said what she had to say.

• • •

Putting your friend's welfare before your own: that was Austen's idea of true friendship. That means admitting when you're wrong, but even more importantly, it means being willing to tell your friend when they are. It took me a long time to wrap my head around that notion, because it flew so strongly in the face of what we believe about friendship today. True friendship, we think, means unconditional acceptance and support. The true friend validates your feelings, takes your side in every argument, helps you feel good about yourself at all times, and never, ever judges you. But Austen didn't believe that. For her, being happy means becoming a better person, and becoming a better person means having your mistakes pointed out to you in a way that you can't ignore. Yes, the true friend wants you to be happy, but being happy and feeling good about yourself are not the same things. In fact, they can sometimes be diametrically opposed. True friends do not shield you from your mistakes, they tell you about them: even at the risk of losing your friendship—which means, even at the risk of being unhappy themselves.

My commitment to this frightening new idea was put to the test the summer after I had finally finished my Austen chapter. My best pal from college had gone off to graduate school in another city, and as the years went by I started to feel as if I knew him less and less. Not because we lost touch, but because he never seemed to say anything real about himself when we were in touch. Not coincidentally, it became more and more clear to me, the few times I did see him, that he was becoming a pretty serious alcoholic.

One weekend he was back in the city, and we arranged a night to catch up. His wife was on his case about the drinking by this point, but she let him out on my recognizance for a harmless beer at the local bar—or so at least we all imagined as the two of us set out.

Well, before we could make it through the initial pleasantries, he had managed to get three drinks down his throat. By about the middle of the second, he had completely checked out of the conversation, at least as far as anything personal was concerned. Before long, I was trying to get the evening over with as quickly as possible and wanted nothing better than to call a cab. But he insisted on driving me home, if only to maintain the pretense that everything was perfectly fine, and I was so afraid of a confrontation that I let him do it.

Then, on the way, he made a wrong turn and ended up— what do you know?—in our old stomping grounds of the East Village. We just had to go to the Blue & Gold for old times' sake, didn't we? So he had another bourbon while I sipped my beer and watched him and wondered what the fuck had happened to the friend I used to know, and then another quick one, and then, what the hell, one more for the road.

We both managed to make it home in one piece, but once my anger wore off, I realized that I had failed him too—not just because I'd let him drive, but because I hadn't had the guts to tell him the truth about himself. Yet we were really still just college buddies, and we simply had no vocabulary with which to talk about anything that grave. I tried to write the next week, starting off all breezy as usual, pretending once again like nothing had happened, but I quickly ground to a halt. There was an elephant in the room that we weren't talking about, and I finally understood that we weren't going to be able to talk about anything else anymore until we did.

It took me another month to screw up the courage to try again. I didn't even tell him that he needed to deal with his drinking. I just told him that I didn't feel like we had a relationship anymore, and that that was really too bad. I knew that he would understand the rest.

Months went by without my hearing from him. I thought our friendship was over. But when he did finally get in touch, it was to tell me he had gotten sober—joined AA and everything—and that my letter had been one of the reasons why. Few things had ever felt better or made me prouder. But as I knew perfectly well, that letter had a coauthor, and it was Austen.

However glad I was that I could be a true friend to someone else, I was even gladder to realize that I had always had one myself. She was that last remaining friend from youth movement, the person who knew me better than I knew myself. The one thing that had always bothered me about her was her tendency to call me on the stupid things I did. Like the time she cut me off—"Billy, she's already heard them all"—before I could make those idiotic puns about her friend Honour's name. She always tried to do it as unobtrusively as possible, but it invariably stung, would make me feel a little small and foolish. Only once I had learned Austen's lessons about humiliation, on the one hand, and friendship, on the other, did I realize how much reason I had to thank my friend for having been on my case for all those years. She had been trying to make me into a presentable person—maybe the person she thought I could be—and she was willing to have faith that it might someday happen.

Predictably, people used to ask me why the two of us didn't get together. The question made me mad. Couldn't men and women be friends without having sex? Apparently not, according to what everyone seemed to believe. I finally did see *When Harry Met Sally . . .* , only to discover that the whole point of the movie was that men and women can't, in fact, be friends, "because the sex thing gets in the way." It was the same wherever I looked. People of the opposite sex might claim to be "just friends," the message was, but count on it, there was always something going on underneath.

The most annoying thing about this apparently universal belief was that it implied that sex was *all* that men and women could really be interested in each other for. Conversation or collaboration or any other kind of common activity seemed to be out of the question. As if we weren't just different genders, but different species.

Well, that was another idea that Austen refused to believe. In fact, as I learned, she was one of the first to challenge it, and she never challenged it more directly than she did in *Persuasion*. Once the people at Lyme got properly introduced to one another, on that visit—Anne and Mary and so forth on the one hand, the Harvilles and Captain Benwick on the other— the heroine always seemed to find herself with Benwick. The two had a lot in common. Both were grieving for lost loves— Anne for Wentworth, Benwick for his fiancée, Captain Harville's late sister. Both were shy, gentle, thoughtful souls. And both, it turned out, were great readers of poetry. Not once or twice, but three times in the space of an evening and a morning—"Anne found Captain Benwick getting near her. . . . Anne found Captain Benwick again drawing near her"—the two young people, both single and unattached, fell into deep, heartfelt conversation about the leading poets of the day, Lord Byron and Sir Walter Scott.

And yet there wasn't the slightest spark, on either side, of sexual interest. Austen was daring us to expect that the two would get together, and she was doing so to teach us a lesson. A man and a woman, even two young, available ones, could talk to each other, understand each other, sympathize with each other, be drawn to each other, even share their intimate thoughts and feelings with each other—as Anne and Benwick did—without having to be attracted to each other—as Anne and Benwick clearly weren't. They could, in other words, be friends.

Nor was Benwick the only man the heroine befriended. Captain Harville was another—someone safer, perhaps, as a married man, but no less unusual as the friend of a woman, and even to this day, almost as liable to raise eyebrows. Their big scene came toward the end of the novel. In the midst of a crowd of other people, Harville, with "the unaffected, easy kindness of manner which denoted the feelings of an older acquaintance than he really was," invited the heroine over for a chat. Their talk soon turned to the relative constancy of the sexes. Who loved longer and with deeper feeling, men or women? The two each argued, of course, for their own side, until Harville produced what he thought to be decisive evidence:

"Let me observe that all histories are against you; all stories, prose and verse. If I had such a memory as Benwick, I could bring you fifty quotations in a moment on my side the argument, and I do not think I ever opened a book in my life which had not something to say upon woman's inconstancy. Songs and proverbs, all talk of woman's fickleness. But perhaps you will say, these were all written by men."

"Perhaps I shall. Yes, yes, if you please, no reference to examples in books. Men have had every advantage of us in telling their own story. Education has been theirs in so much higher a degree; the pen has been in their hands. I will not allow books to prove anything."

"The pen has been in their hands": but not, of course, any-more. The moment was exhilarating—Austen's crowning declaration as a writer, the feminist flag she planted on the ground of English fiction. But the scene did not just make a feminist argument, it *was* a feminist argument. Anne and Harville shared a common footing in the conversation, debating each other with mutual respect and affection and esteem. Men and women can be equals, Austen was telling us, so men and women can be friends.

Fortunately, blessedly, I already knew that. (It was one of the things I had learned in youth movement.) And it was through that same best friend that I began at last to be drawn into the kind of friendship circle, the kind of floating community, for which I'd been longing for so many years. She had a friend from graduate school whose family owned a place in New England—the sweetest old house you could imagine, with a wide front porch that opened up like a grandmother's lap and a big, cozy living room where they used to hold the dances when the place belonged to the town. The kitchen clock was stopped at 10:36—the perfect time, we used to joke, A.M. or P.M.—not too early and not too late.

The situation bore uncanny resemblances to *Persuasion*. The house was by the water, like Lyme. (In fact, it wasn't far from Lyme—the one in Connecticut.) The guy whose family owned it was a sailor, with a sailor's bluff practicality and the kind of unpretentious warmth that so delighted Anne among the people of the navy. Like the Harvilles, he invited from the heart. Like the Harvilles, he accommodated as many friends as wanted to come, and anyone who came became a friend. Like the Harvilles, in short, he made you feel at home.

On weekends when the weather was mild, his friends would be drawn to the place from all over the Northeast. I would come up from the city, my friend would drive down from New Hampshire, a few Connecticut people would stop by, and we'd spend the weekend just being lazy and silly together. The light would slant in from the water, the gulls would call and circle overhead, we'd pass the days playing ball and eating clams, the nights drinking beer, playing guitar, and talking, talking, talking. As time went on, we became as comfortable with one another as a pair of old shoes. We listened to one another's stories, met one another's boyfriends and girlfriends, and tolerated and even grew fond of one another's faults.

We were all drawn there for the same reasons, all feeling that sense of loss that comes, in your early thirties, when you've fi-nally separated from your parents. Some of us were already paired up in long-term relationships, some of us weren't—it didn't matter, in that sense. In another sense, of course, it mat-tered very much. So when, the autumn after I finished my Aus-ten chapter, our host fell suddenly and deeply in love, we all came up one weekend—they were already living together, it happened so fast—to meet his girlfriend.

There were about eight of us sitting around the kitchen table that night, smacking our lips over some dessert she had made. The candles were burning low, her cats were nosing their way among our legs, someone had just cracked a joke. I leaned back, I looked around, and I thought, *Yes, I've found my family.*

CHAPTER 6

sense and sensibility
falling in love

I had now been in Brooklyn for nearly three years, and I had a great deal to be thankful for. I had worked out a way of dealing with my father that enabled us to have a reasonably positive relationship. I no longer worried about his approval, and I had come to accept the fact that he was never going to change. Having completed my Austen chapter and written some hundred pages on *Middlemarch*, I was more than halfway through the dissertation and was beginning to think I might actually finish someday. And I had found my way to a real circle of friends.

But one thing was still missing. One big, huge thing. I hadn't found anyone to be with. Not just sleep with, but be with. Not just a hookup, or a short-lived affair, or a summer fling, but a real, stable, satisfying relationship. Coming out of youth movement and college and the first few years of graduate school—sheltered spaces, all of them, that made it relatively easy to find a girlfriend—I was unprepared for the full horror of the New York dating scene. It was like entering an endless maze of stupid conversations, as confusing as the subway and equally bleak. Instead of meeting people through friends, like I always had, I was expected to endear myself to complete strangers—who knew exactly what I was trying to do—in the time it took to walk into a party or order a drink.

And this being New York, it wasn't enough to be charming (not that I had a clue any longer about how to be charming). You had to be impressive, you had to look successful, you had to sound like a winner, especially as a man. What did you do? Who did you know? Where had you gone to school? I learned to drop the salient points of my résumé into the first five minutes of a conversation. It got so that talking to single women felt like having a job interview. Just be yourself, people would say. Be myself? Wasn't that the whole problem?

I was spared no indignity. Blind dates. Setups. A dinner invitation from a woman who turned out to have a boyfriend and "didn't realize this was a date." A parade of women who liked me, but "not in that way." "At least you've made a new friend!" my friends would say. "I don't want any more goddamn friends!" I would shoot back.

One day, I struck up a conversation with a woman on the way out of exercise class—one of those miraculous situations where you're already in the middle before you have a chance to feel nervous. She was smart, nice, interesting, pretty. When we got to the corner and seemed about to go our separate ways, we turned to each other at the same time and said, "So what's your name?"

Her name was Pam. Pam, Pam, Pam, Pam, Pam. I thought

about seeing her again all week. But the next week came, and she didn't show up. I started to get a little desperate. Surely she would come back the following week. But she wasn't there the following week, either. Finally, I got so distraught that I put one of those "missed connections" ads in the *Village Voice*: "Desperately Seeking Pam," with the place and date and my phone number.

Here's a tip: don't put your number in a personal ad. First I got a call from a woman pretending to be Pam ("Of course I'm Pam"—"Okay, so what do you do for a living?"—"Oh, c'mon"). Then I got a call from a woman who admitted that she wasn't Pam but was hoping we could get together anyway. Then I got a call from a guy in New Jersey who wanted to commiserate about how hard it was to meet women. ("Maybe you should stop going to those singles events with your richer, better-looking friend," I suggested.) Then I got a call from a *guy* pretending to be Pam. ("You can call me Pam if you want to.") And finally, late at night, I got one last call from a guy with a voice like sandpaper, who let me know that, for the right price, he'd be happy to introduce me to "Pam."

I did have one serious relationship during those years. It all started very romantically. I met her at the wedding of an old friend. Actually, as I discovered later, it had been a setup. She had chosen me out of a whole lineup of eligible guys that my friend had laid out—literally, with pictures—upon her request. Well, a short lineup. Okay, me and another guy. But still. It made it all seem even more romantic, when she told me—like the whole thing was meant to be.

My friend arranged to have her pick me up at the airport bus, and as I climbed into the car, we felt the chemistry right away—not just sexual sparks, but an immediate feeling of ease and familiarity and kinship, as if we already knew each other and were merely resuming a conversation that had gotten briefly interrupted. We were inseparable the entire weekend, didn't stop laughing, couldn't believe our luck. The wedding was in Michigan (she and my friend had just finished a graduate program together at the U of M), and when she set out for Boston right after the ceremony to start a new job, a new life, she invited me along for the ride—a spur-of-the-moment dash that seemed to have all the glamour and daring of Bonnie and Clyde making a getaway.

We traded stories the whole way, spent the night at a motel in Niagara Falls, of all places (we hadn't even realized that it was a honeymoon spot), and as I tore myself away from her a couple of days later, swore that we were committed to making the relationship succeed, even though it was going to have to be conducted long-distance. We even mentioned the M-word—as in, "Yes, I think I would be ready to get married if things work out." That sentence actually came out of my mouth. I couldn't believe how grown up I was being. It felt like all that Austen was paying off, and that now I was ready for a mature, adult romance.

Well, it didn't take long for things to go south. Fights in Boston, fights in Brooklyn, fights over e-mail (which had just come in). Fights about my feelings, fights about her feelings, fights about the fights we'd just had. Fights that spun off little subsidiary fights that had to be resolved before we could get back to the main fight. Endless phone calls where we'd talk for a few minutes until we stumbled over something to fight about, then spend the rest of the evening fighting about it.

I was so in love with the idea of having a mature relationship, of throwing around words like *married,* that I forgot to ask myself whether I was actually happy with this person. The truth was, we weren't really compatible—didn't, once the honeymoon phase was over and we started to get to know each other for real, even much like each other. But it took me months to finally give up and admit it, because I was still under the spell of that romantic beginning, the allure of the story we would one day get to tell.

Once it was over, I almost swore off serious relationships altogether. The meeting, the spark, the sense of kinship: wasn't that what love was supposed to look like? Were my instincts that bad? And what if I hadn't gotten out before it was too late? It was an awfully narrow escape. For someone as allergic to commitment as I was, the experience was chilling. I still wanted to find a girlfriend, I finally decided, but I was more determined than ever not to let myself get married.

Having long since finished my first chapter, I thought I was done with Austen for a while, but that was the year that all those adaptations started to come out: *Clueless, Persuasion,* the Colin Firth *Pride and Prejudice,* the Gwyneth Paltrow *Emma.* My favorite, though, was the Ang Lee/Emma Thompson adaptation of *Sense and Sensibility*. It was light, it was charming, it was fun—qualities I had never associated with the book itself. *Sense and Sensibility*, like *Persuasion* and *Mansfield Park*, belonged to the darker wing of Austen's fiction. It was a sober, even bitter book—satiric but not joyful, funny but not comic. It contained my single favorite line in all of Austen—"She was not a woman of many words; for, unlike people in general, she proportioned them to the number of her ideas" (a double-edged piece of irony that left no one standing and pretty much epitomized the book's disposition)—but the novel as a whole had never won me over.

Now I went back to it again, to see how such a delightful movie could have been produced from so frustrating a book. My problem with *Sense and Sensibility* was the same as the one I had had with *Mansfield Park*: it wanted us to accept something that I refused to believe—something that I had trouble accepting even Austen believed. The story seemed perversely unromantic, even anti-romantic. *Sense and Sensibility* set two visions of love before us, each exemplified through one of its heroines, and insisted that we prefer the less appealing.

Marianne Dashwood was everything that you could want in a romantic heroine. She was young, beautiful, passionate, and unreserved. She sang like an angel, read poetry with feeling, and took long, solitary rambles at twilight. Her ideas of love were high and exacting. "The more I know of the world," she said, "the more am I convinced that I shall never see a man whom I can really love." Not only would such a man need virtue and intelligence, but his figure would have to be striking, his eyes full of spirit and fire. And to be worthy of her passion, something still more was required. "I could not be happy with a man whose taste did not in every point coincide with my own. He must enter into all my feelings; the same books, the same music must charm us both." Marianne was not just looking for a husband; she was seeking a soul mate.

Amazingly, such a man soon appeared. Running home one blustery morning to escape the rain, Marianne fell and twisted her ankle. Out of nowhere, it seemed, a gentleman rushed to her rescue, sweeping her up in his arms and carrying her to safety. He was young, handsome, elegant, and manly. His manner was charming, his voice expressive, his movements graceful. What was more, it soon turned out, he shared all of Marianne's passions: for music and poetry, dancing and riding. Fate, it seemed, had destined them for one another. Before long, Marianne had come to feel that she understood this man as well as she knew herself. "It is not time or opportunity that is to determine intimacy," she said, "it is disposition alone. Seven years would be insufficient to make some people acquainted with each other, and seven days are more than enough for others." His name was Willoughby, and they fell quickly and deeply in love.

Her older sister, Elinor, meanwhile, was involved in a romance of her own—if you could call it that. As the novel opened, the heroines were about to lose their childhood home of Norland. Their father had died, and they and their mother and younger sister were going to be displaced by their half brother, John, and his wife, Fanny. John "was not an ill-disposed young man, unless to be rather cold hearted, and rather selfish, is to be ill-disposed," and Fanny was even worse. He might have allowed the Dashwood women to remain at Norland, if only grudgingly, but she was determined to send them packing, especially once Elinor had struck up a friendship with her brother Edward.

Bland and halting and practically paralyzed by shyness, with no conspicuous talents and no particular ambitions, Edward was the very opposite of Willoughby, and no one's idea of a lover. The poor guy wasn't even handsome. But then again, Elinor was not exactly going to set the world on fire herself. Prudent where Marianne was passionate, merely pretty where she was beautiful, proper where her sister scorned conventional expectations, she did everything she could to restrain and downplay her feelings (and caution Marianne about not running away with her own). She and Edward had become friends, but their attachment hardly seemed to go any deeper than that.

In what counted for Elinor as an unguarded moment, she admitted to her sister that, as she put it in her typically schoolmarmish way, "I have seen a great deal of him, have studied his sentiments, and heard his opinion on subjects of literature and taste; and, upon the whole, I venture to pronounce that his mind is well-informed, his enjoyment of books exceedingly great, his imagination lively, his observation just and correct, and his taste delicate and pure." It was a wonder that she managed to stay awake until the end of the sentence. Pressed a little harder, she rose to what passed with her for passion: "I do not attempt to deny that I think very highly of him—that I greatly esteem, that I like him." She seemed to be willing to use every word but the one we wanted to hear. "Esteem him! Like him!" Marianne replied, as if she were reading our minds. "Use those words again, and I will leave the room this moment."

* * *

And yet it was Elinor and Edward's tepid relationship, not Marianne and Willoughby's wild, impassioned romance, that turned out to be the novel's idea of true love. Elinor's way was validated, as the plot went on to unfold, Marianne's discredited. I understood, of course, from having absorbed Austen's lessons about growing up, that Marianne put too much faith in her feelings, was too much of a capital-R Romantic. It took her seven exclamation points, after all, just to say good-bye to their old house. ("Dear, dear Norland! . . . when shall I cease to regret you! . . . Oh! happy house!") Yes, Marianne was often made to look naïve and overwrought, but that only told me how biased Austen was against her, as well as how hard the author needed to work to convince us—at times, it seemed, to convince herself—of the superiority of Elinor's version of love. I knew that Austen wanted us to place reason over feeling, but choosing Elinor-love over Marianne-love was not about doing that. It was about choosing between two *kinds* of feeling, two notions of what love really means.

When we think about love, we think about Romeo and Juliet, that idea of romance—just as they did in Austen's day, just as they did in Shakespeare's day, just as we always have and always will. We believe, like Marianne, in love at first sight. She scarcely had an opportunity to even glance at her rescuer, that very first day, but she saw enough to know that "his person and air were equal to what her fancy had ever drawn for the hero of a favourite story," and she thirsted to learn all about him. A second meeting, the next day, only confirmed what she already felt. Like Michael Corleone in *The Godfather,* Marianne had been hit with "the thunderbolt."

We also believe, like Marianne, that true love happens only once. Marianne was staunchly against second attachments, as they called them at the time, and thus, second marriages. Shorter life expectancies made second unions as normal in Austen's day as divorce makes them in our own. Of course, we're free today, as Marianne and her contemporaries certainly were not, to have as many relationships, marital or otherwise, as we want. But while we may not put the matter quite as squarely as she did, we tend to believe that only the last, only the one we finally arrive at, is the real thing. All the others were mistakes. Marianne believed that just the first connection counted, we believe that just the last one does, but we both agree that true love is a one-time thing.

Despite the way our lives have changed, we also still believe, like Marianne, in young love. At least, to judge from a host of books and songs and movies, we want to believe in it. Juliet was thirteen, not because people married that young in Shakespeare's day—they didn't—but because we have always imagined that true love is inseparable from the ardor and freshness and innocence of youth. Love, we think, is springtime and beginnings. Marianne was sixteen, Austen's youngest heroine. For her, "a woman of seven-and-twenty can never hope to feel or inspire affection again"—exactly what everyone thought about Anne Elliot in *Persuasion,* too—and a man of thirty-five "must have long outlived every sensation of the kind." If we no longer agree with Marianne's arithmetic, it is not because we have changed our ideas about love; it is because we feel young and stay young for so much longer than people did in Austen's day.

We believe in soul mates, believe that there is one true love out there for us in the world and that the stars will guide her to us. In Yiddish, they call that person your *bashert,* your destiny. Of all the myths of love that have come down to us from ancient Greece, the one that we cherish the most is the story told by Plato, that humans were originally one creature with four arms and four legs, and that the gods separated us because we were too powerful in that idyllic state. Now we roam the world, looking for our other half and seeking to reunite our bodies in love. "You complete me," we say, reflecting the same kind of feeling.

And so, like Marianne, we think that true love means perfect agreement in taste and perfect freedom from conflict—ideas embodied in the dating sites, with their careful alignment of personal characteristics and their names like Perfect Match and eHarmony. The true lover, we think, is a second self. And thus, conversely, the loss of love is tantamount to death. Romeo, believing that Juliet was dead, committed suicide; Juliet, awakened from her deathlike slumber, ended her own life in turn.

Marianne came close to suffering the same fate. After weeks of bliss, her great affair quite suddenly collapsed, and it almost took her with it. One day Willoughby was about to propose, the next he was gone without a trace. Marianne was thrown into a fever of anxiety: what could it mean? She followed him to London, sent note after note, refused to tell her sister what was going on, and finally tracked him down at a ball, only to be jilted in the most public and brutal way (for reasons we discover only later). Now the heroine lost all interest in life, spiraling into depression and openly courting the illness that almost killed her. If there was only one true love for her, and it was gone, then what was left to live for?

Love, we think, is something that happens *to* us, a force that comes upon us unawares and makes of us its plaything. It acts without regard to our intentions, cares nothing for our welfare, bends our will to its own. Cupid shoots his arrow out of a clear blue sky, driving us mad with desire. In Dante's *Inferno*, Paolo and Francesca, the first and most sympathetic of the sinners, are whirled about by Love like particles in a force field, helpless before its power. In Greek myth, love literally tears people apart. Love is not just a god but the greatest of the gods, before whom even the others are helpless. Like a flame, it consumes everything in its path.

And thus we feel, like Marianne, that true love is wild and free, that it knows no bounds or rules. We skip classes, make love outdoors, take crazy risks that turn us into people our friends don't recognize. When Marianne and Willoughby first got together—this was what frightened her sister the most— they threw propriety to the wind, shamelessly displaying their intimacy for all to see, neglecting their obligations toward their neighbors (and laughing behind their backs about it), driving alone around the countryside in the most scandalous way. For Marianne—as for Romeo and Juliet, who came from feuding clans, and Paolo and Francesca, who committed adultery—true love proves itself by overrunning conventional boundaries and norms. It is, by its very nature, illicit, dangerous, rebellious.

. . .

I could certainly relate to what Marianne was going through. I had once felt something like it myself, the summer I was eighteen. It happened at camp, in youth movement, but it didn't even wait until we got to camp to start. We were milling around the movement office in New York, waiting for the bus to take us up, when I rounded a corner and felt my face go hot. My body must've gotten the message before my brain figured out what was happening. There she was, sitting on a desk like she'd been waiting for me, the most beautiful girl I had ever seen— no, the *only* girl I had ever seen. "Hi!" she said, with a smile like the blue sky. "Hi," I replied, beating an unsteady retreat, kind of blown back by the power of it all and not exactly sure where my arms and legs were at the moment.

But I had managed, in that split second, to catch a look on her face that told me that it wasn't a question of if, but when. After that, no matter where I was—on the bus ride up, during our first few days at camp—it felt as though I had a rope coming out of the back of my head that was connected to wherever she happened to be, as if she were always somehow standing right behind me. It didn't take long before we started spending an awful lot of time together. My heart had stopped flopping around quite so clumsily by then and we seemed to be drawn together by a kind of gravitational pull. Without ever planning it, we always just happened to end up sitting together, or walking together, or finally—well, finally, we became a couple.

I was eighteen, for God's sake. There was nothing but her

face, nothing but her eyes. The summer held its breath for us. I'd never said "I love you" before, and now it seemed beside the point to ever say anything else. I walked around in a trance: I couldn't believe that anything could feel so strong, feel so pure. We kissed until our lips were chapped. One afternoon, we were sitting there beneath an apple tree. "Do you ever feel like we're the same person?" I said. She looked down. She looked up. "Yes," she said.

The summer breathed out: it was over. Camp was over; life was over. I felt like I was splitting apart, like there was a hole between my arms where her body was supposed to be. She was from Texas, and still in high school. We'd never said it out loud, but we both knew that we'd come to the end. We had no e-mail, of course, no long-distance, no control over our lives and no hope of seeing each other again. Even writing seemed beside the point. The only thing that didn't seem beside the point was curling up in a ball and trying to disappear.

So I completely sympathized with Marianne. Like everyone else, I believed in her idea of love, and it drove me crazy that Austen didn't seem to. Or at least, she didn't seem to in *Sense and Sensibility*. Weren't her other books incredibly romantic? Was I missing something here?

The movie of the novel only left me more perplexed. How *had* the filmmakers managed to endow the same story with so much feeling? When I went back and looked more carefully, I realized how: by cheating. They didn't change Marianne and Willoughby's story—they didn't need to—but they sure changed

Elinor and Edward's. They gave Edward an adorably dry sense of humor. They gave him a sweet, big-brotherly relationship with Margaret, the youngest Dashwood sister, who scarcely appeared in the novel as more than a name. Of course, they also had him played by Hugh Grant, who not only bumbles more charmingly than anyone since Jimmy Stewart, but who's as handsome as they come. And by granting Elinor herself a new depth of feeling—taking leave of Norland, she stroked a horse in pensive farewell, a scene that was absent from the novel— they made that character lovable, too.

The same went for the other match that ended the story— which was, in the book, even more unromantic than Elinor and Edward's. In Austen's version Marianne was more or less forced to marry a man she had just begun to like and certainly didn't love, and the whole business was dispatched, as a kind of afterthought, in barely more than a page, as if to openly defy our resistance. But the movie borrowed flourishes from Austen's other books—the surprise gift of a piano from *Emma,* the murmuring of verse à deux from *Persuasion*—to give the thing the lineaments of romance.

Now it was easy to see why both couples would fall in love. But that only left me more puzzled as to why Austen had made it so hard. The novel may have been an early effort, but it wasn't as if she lacked the means—or desire—to write a ravishing love story at that point in her career. She had already written *Pride and Prejudice,* her most devastating romance of all.

And then I finally remembered two things. One was *Mansfield Park,* the other novel that had seemed to stand against everything that I thought Austen believed. The other was my relationship with the woman I had met at the wedding in Michigan. Of course, I thought. How could I have been so blind? I had just *had* a Marianne-and-Willoughby romance, and it had crashed and burned in no time flat. Fate, soul mates, love at first sight, throwing caution to the wind—it had had all the elements, adhered to all the myths, and it had all been totally wrong.

Maybe the problem, I finally realized, was the myths. Marianne thought that Willoughby reminded her of the heroes of her favorite stories, and I had clung to that relationship because the way it started seemed like something from a movie. We had both been deluded by our expectations about what love was supposed to look like. It was *Northanger Abbey* all over again: conventional beliefs, derived from fiction, that turned out to bear no relationship to reality.

But didn't Austen's other books promote those same beliefs? Now that I really thought about what made them feel romantic, I saw to my chagrin that the answer was no. She made us adore her heroines and admire her heroes, made us long to see them get together, devised ingenious ways to keep them apart and finally unite them, teased us with a whole array of traps and feints and surprises, but search as I might, I could never find a single one of those clichés in which I'd put such faith.

I had simply imposed my ideas of romance on Austen's novels without really thinking about it—just as the people who make those adaptations always seem to do. The Keira Knightley *Pride and Prejudice* may not alter the basic story, but it does embellish it with all the trappings of movie love: swelling music, windswept vistas, glowing sunsets. Elizabeth strikes moody poses, her lover strides towards her through waving fields of grass, the two lock lips with hungry urgency. But why shouldn't they? The young woman whom Mr. Darcy called "tolerable, but not handsome enough to tempt *me*" is drop-dead gorgeous now. Patricia Rozema's travesty of *Mansfield Park* (the one with Harold Pinter as Sir Thomas) turns prudish little Fanny Price into a naughty and bold young rebel with teasing eyes and a sensuous mouth. The 1995 *Persuasion* ends, unthinkably, with a public, premarital kiss. Even the Colin Firth *Pride and Prejudice,* more faithful to Austen than most, plunges the overheated hero into the water (a sigh goes up around the world) in scarcely more than his skivvies.

But Austen, of course, was way ahead of us. She knew what we'd be thinking, and in *Sense and Sensibility,* I now saw, she headed us off at the pass. Which was where *Mansfield Park* came in. That novel told us something essential—that goodness was more important than wit—that her other books allowed us to miss. And it did so by separating the two qualities into different characters (Fanny on the one hand, Mary Crawford on the other) and challenging us to go against our instincts as to which one we ought to prefer. So it was, I now saw, here. Austen's other novels were all so romantic in obvious ways that we didn't need to pay attention to what *really* made them so. Now, by putting the two on different sides, she forced us to tell them apart. Elinor was to Marianne what Fanny was to Mary Crawford: the less appealing choice, but the right one. Marianne got the storybook romance; Elinor got what Austen called true love.

•   •   •

Once I opened my mind to this possibility, it started to make perfect sense. For Elinor-love—and Elizabeth-love and Emma-love and love in all the other novels, now that I really thought about it—was perfectly consistent with everything else I'd learned from Austen: about goodness, about growing up, about learning, about friendship.

For her, I saw, love is not something that happens *to* you, suddenly or otherwise; it's something you have to prepare yourself for. As long as Elizabeth thought that she was right about everything, as long as Emma disdained the people around her, as long as Marianne ignored her sister's advice about the things she owed her neighbors and family, their hearts remained closed. For Austen, before you can fall in love with someone else, you have to come to know yourself. In other words, you have to grow up. Love isn't going to magically transform you, make you into a better or even a different person—another myth that I'd bought into—it can only work with what you already are.

Like it said in *Northanger Abbey,* we have to learn to love. I knew those words applied to loving things like hyacinths or novels, but I never really thought that they applied to, you know, *love* love, romantically loving another person. What could be more natural than falling in love? Strange as it seemed, however, Austen was saying that we aren't actually born knowing how. Youth is not a necessity in her idea of romance; it's an impediment. Yes, most of her heroines were quite young by our standards, but by the time they fell in love, they had shed their innocence and ignorance. One, of course, was even as old as Marianne's dreaded twenty-seven, and two of Austen's heroes were at least thirty-five. As for Marianne herself, she began the novel at sixteen but ended it some three years older—as old as her sister, and finally as wise, as when the story started.

But knowing yourself, Austen taught me, is not enough. You also need to know the person you fall in love with, and despite what Marianne and I believed, this doesn't happen overnight. To Austen, love at first sight is a contradiction in terms. Lust at first sight, a whole train of fantasies and projections at first sight—those she recognized. But love at first sight, never. As dull as it sounded, I now saw, Elinor's way of going about things is the right one: to see a great deal of a person, to study their sentiments, to hear their opinions. Needless to say, neither a moment nor a week can suffice for such an operation; only a long, patient acquaintance is enough. A person's character, as Marianne—and Elizabeth Bennet, and I myself—all discovered to our sorrow, could not be read at a glance. And it is a person's character, not their body, with which we fall in love.

None of this happens rationally, though, as if you drew up a checklist of pros and cons—another cinematic cliché—and toted up the sum. Elinor's way, I recognized, is every bit as intuitive as Marianne's, and, if anything, takes place at a deeper level. Not only does love not strike you in an instant, it turned out, it doesn't even "strike" you at all. You never know the moment that you fall in love, in Austen's vision; you only discover you already have. "Will you tell me how long you have loved him?" Elizabeth was asked near the end of *Pride and Prejudice*.

"It has been coming on so gradually," she replied, "that I hardly know when it began." As for Elinor and Edward, I realized, we never even heard about it. At one point it was "like," at another it was "love," and Austen simply trusted us to understand that the first had slowly turned into the second.

So, I asked myself, what if Elinor and Edward had never met? What if she had "seen a great deal" of someone else? What if she had discovered that *his* mind was well informed, *his* observation just and correct, *his* taste delicate and pure? Would she have fallen in love with him, instead? Austen's reply was brutally clear: of course she would have. There is no "one person" out there, Elinor's creator was trying to tell us. Austen had no use, I saw, for things like fate or soul mates, second selves or other halves, guiding stars or Greek myths, or any other of the mystical ideas with which we try to turn love into something cosmic, something sacred, something more than what it is: a relationship dependent, at least in its inception, not on destiny but on its very opposite—chance.

And then, I realized, she went a terrible step further. Even once we fall in love, she said, it isn't necessarily forever. Divorce was not a realistic possibility in Austen's world, but death and disenchantment both were, and when they occurred, she thought, it was perfectly possible—even inevitable—to fall in love a second time. "He will rally again," Anne Elliot believed of Captain Benwick in *Persuasion,* just lately bereaved of his fiancée, "and be happy with another." Benwick himself did not believe it, but so it proved to be, and faster than even Anne had imagined. As for Marianne, instead of dying for love, as she first expected, or withdrawing from the world, as she later planned, she lived to form the thing that had not been dreamt of in her philosophy, a second attachment.

"The cure of unconquerable passions, and the transfer of unchanging attachments," wrote the grandmother of romance fiction, the author who launched a score of sappy movies and a hundred sentimental sequels, "must vary much as to time in different people." No passions, in other words, are unconquerable, no attachments exist that can't be transferred. Our hearts can change, just like our minds. Austen believed in love, I saw; she just did not believe in it the way we want her to.

None of this was merely theoretical for her. Austen was called upon to give some real-life romantic advice at a certain point, and she put her money where her mouth was. When Fanny Knight, her favorite niece, was twenty-one, she was trying to decide whether to marry a local young gentleman, John Plumptre. The young lady had her doubts. He seemed a little stiff, a little too religious and moralistic, and in any case, she wasn't sure that she loved him enough. So in the course of two long exchanges, she hashed it all out with her wise Aunt Jane.

The correspondence was top secret: Fanny concealed the first letter in a package of sheet music, and even Austen's sister, Cassandra, was not allowed to be in on it. "I do not know how I could have accounted for the parcel otherwise," Austen said approvingly, "for tho' your dear Papa most conscientiously hunted about till he found me alone in the Dining-parlor, Your Aunt C. had seen that he *had* a parcel to deliver.—As it was however, I do not think anything was suspected." The second letter, though, began to make her sweat. "I shall be most glad to hear from you again my dearest Fanny," she said, "but . . . write *something* that may do to be read"—that is, read aloud—"or told."

Austen examined the letters, as may be imagined, with keen attention. "I read yours through the very evening I received it," she replied, "getting away by myself—I could not bear to leave off, when once I had begun." This was no mean trick in such a tight-knit household, with three other women— Cassandra, their mother, and Austen's best friend, Martha Lloyd—breathing down her neck. "Luckily," she explained, "Your Aunt C. dined at the other house, therefore I had not to manoeuvre away from *her*;—& as to anybody else, I do not care."

Austen's response to her niece's dilemma, however, was more ambivalent. "My dearest Fanny," she interrupted herself at one point, "I am writing what will not be of the smallest use to you. I am feeling differently every moment, & shall not be able to suggest a single thing that can assist your Mind." Fanny quite plainly felt otherwise, though, and in talking out the arguments on both sides of the question, Austen not only helped her niece reach a decision, she affirmed the romantic beliefs that her own novels expressed. What she urged on her readers was good enough for her own flesh and blood.

The problem was this. On the one hand, Mr. Plumptre was clearly a very worthy young man. On the other, Fanny's affection for him, as Austen saw, was already on the decline. But as she consoled her niece, by reflecting on the young man's qualities, for having made the mistake of thinking herself in love in the first place, Austen's mind began to change once more:

Oh! my dear Fanny, the more I write about him, the warmer my feelings become, the more strongly I feel the sterling worth of such a young Man & the desirableness of your growing in love with him again. I recommend this most thoroughly.—There are such beings in the World perhaps, one in a Thousand, as the Creature You & I should think perfection, where Grace & Spirit are united to Worth, where the Manners are equal to the Heart & Understanding, but such a person may not come in your way.

In choosing a mate, she was telling her niece, the most important thing is character. Grace and spirit and manners—the kinds of qualities that attracted Marianne to Willoughby—are wonderful to have, but they are no substitute for the Edward-like attributes of worth and heart and understanding. All of Austen's heroes had the second; only a couple were also blessed with the first.

Yet talking Fanny into the match was the last thing that Austen wanted to do. "You frighten me out of my Wits," she said at one point. "Your affection gives me the highest pleasure, but indeed you must not let anything depend on my opinion. Your feelings & none but your own, should determine such an important point." Feelings, not arguments. You shouldn't marry someone because of his character; you should marry him because of the emotions that his character inspires. "Anything is to be preferred or endured rather than marrying without Affection," Austen reminded her niece, "and nothing can be compared to the misery of being bound *without* Love."

Still, feelings can change, and we can do something about it. "The desirableness of your growing in love with him again": it sounded like Austen were asking her niece to perform the impossible. Surely you can no more choose to grow in love than you can decide to grow taller. Yet Austen believed that if a person's character is good, love increases with simple familiarity. She said "grow," not "fall"—a gradual, organic process, not a bolt from the blue. "I should not be afraid of your *marrying* him," she explained; "with all his Worth, you would soon love him enough for the happiness of both."

"*Marrying*" as opposed to becoming engaged to. The problem was that Mr. Plumptre's financial circumstances were not going to allow the two of them to formalize their union anytime soon. "You like him well enough to marry," Austen told her niece, "but not well enough to wait." Love, again, depends on chance—and in more ways than one. No, the perfect man may never arrive, but Fanny was only twenty-one, and, Austen insisted,

> When I consider how few young Men you have yet seen much of—how capable you are (yes, I do still think you very capable) of being really in love—how full of temptation the next 6 or 7 years of your Life will probably be—(it is the very period of Life for the strongest attachments to be formed)—I cannot wish you with your present very cool feelings to devote yourself in honour to him.

What was more, "It is very true that you never may attach another Man, his equal altogether, but if that other Man has the power of attaching you *more,* he will be in your eyes the most perfect."

Better to love than be loved—something we never had to learn from the novels, where feelings, by authorial grace, were always perfectly reciprocal. As for "Poor dear Mr. J. P.," Austen said, "I have no doubt of his suffering a good deal for a time, a great deal, when he feels that he must give you up;—but it is no creed of mine, as you must be well aware, that such sort of Disappointments kill anybody." As it turned out, Fanny took her aunt's advice, and nobody died. John Plumptre married three years later, had three daughters, and approved of *Mansfield Park,* on account of its stern morality. Fanny waited six years, just as her aunt suggested, married a man a dozen years her senior with six children from a first marriage, and had nine more kids of her own.

Austen was not against romance, she was against romantic mythology. No one who wrote as many novels about love and marriage as she did can fairly be accused of being unromantic. If anything, simply believing that people should marry for love, that "nothing can be compared to the misery of being bound *without* Love," made her all too romantic by the standards of the day. People wrote stories of crazy love, then as now, and some people, especially young people, believed them, but when it came time to lay it on the line and commit themselves for life, most were far more apt to forget about love altogether.

Those were the days of the marriage market, when young people were auctioned off according to a strict system of equivalences. Men offered money and status, women offered money, if they had any, and beauty, and the exchange rates were calculated to a hair. Here was Elinor and Marianne's odious half brother, John Dashwood, who would never have dreamed of marrying for love, handicapping the heroines' chances. Elinor had just informed him that her sister (in the wake of Willoughby's rejection) had taken ill:

> I am sorry for that. At her time of life, any thing of an illness destroys the bloom for ever! Her's has been a very short one! She was as handsome a girl last September, as any I ever saw; and as likely to attract the men. . . . I remember Fanny [his wife] used to say that she would marry sooner and better than you did. . . . She will be mistaken, however. I question whether Marianne now, will marry a man worth more than five or six hundred a year, at the utmost, and I am very much deceived if you do not do better.

The worst thing about this system was that no one forced you into it. Parents could pressure their children not to "marry down," could disown them for doing it or even thinking of doing it, but the days of arranged marriages were long over. Young people had a choice, and made a choice, but so thoroughly had they internalized the values of the marriage market—marry prudently, marry "well," don't worry about love—that they acted just as if their parents still decided for them.

"Happiness in marriage is entirely a matter of chance," said one of Austen's young ladies, "and it is better to know as little as possible of the defects of the person with whom you are to pass your life." "There is not one in a hundred of either sex who is not taken in when they marry," said another. "It is a manoeuvring business," "of all transactions, the one in which people expect most from others, and are least honest themselves." If happiness was simply a matter of chance, if marriage was just a maneuvering business, then you might as well go for the gold.

This kind of attitude, as much as the romantic dreams of a Marianne Dashwood, was what Austen wrote her novels to rebuke. The first of those young ladies was Elizabeth Bennet's friend Charlotte, who went on to marry the most ridiculous— and surely, for a wife, the most distasteful—man in the world. "I am not romantic," she explained; "I never was. I ask only a comfortable home; and considering Mr. Collins's character, connection, and situation in life"—yes, *that* Mr. Collins, one of the greatest fools in English literature—"I am convinced that my chance of happiness with him is as fair as most people can boast on entering the marriage state." No doubt. The second young lady was Mary Crawford in *Mansfield Park,* who couldn't bring herself to marry the man she loved. Two versions, for their creator, of self-damnation.

Austen was no fool. She neither demonized wealth nor idealized poverty. Among the factors weighing in Mr. Plumptre's favor, she told her niece when she gave her romantic advice, was that he was "the eldest son of a Man of Fortune." He may not have had much money yet, in other words, but he was going to have an awful lot eventually. "What have wealth or grandeur to do with happiness?" said Marianne, in high romantic mode. To which her older sister replied, "Grandeur has but little, but wealth has much to do with it." All that Austen claimed—it was revolutionary enough, if put into practice—was that wealth can be no substitute for love.

In fact, her heroines did put it into practice, and so did she. Fanny Price, in *Mansfield Park,* turned down a match that would have made her rich. Elizabeth Bennet, in *Pride and Prejudice,* turned down two. Austen's niece—as the daughter of Austen's wealthy brother Edward, a young woman accustomed to a style of life that only marrying very well would have allowed her to maintain—turned down that "eldest son of a Man of Fortune" on her aunt's advice. And Austen herself, coming to the end of her chances for any kind of match at all, turned down the hand of Harris Bigg-Wither (her friends' brother, the man whose offer she accepted just a few days shy of her twenty-seventh birthday, only to change her mind that very night), who was also the heir to a large fortune—a man who would have made her rich indeed.

The stakes, in those decisions, could not have been higher. For Fanny Price, for Elizabeth Bennet, and most of all, for Austen herself, accepting the man in question would not only have saved them from lives of deprivation and insecurity, it would have gone a long way toward saving their families, too. By marrying Harris, as Austen biographer Claire Tomalin put it, Austen would have been able "to ensure the comfort of her parents to the end of their days, and give a home to Cassandra," and she would probably also have been in a position to help her brothers in their careers. She would have become a benefactor rather than a dependent, a great lady instead of a poor relation. And yet, despite it all, she didn't do it. She valued love too much: real love, not storybook love. Valued it enough not to profane it for comfort's sake, and to devote her career to defending it.

What about sex? Jane Austen the prudish spinster is a figure of legend and nothing more. The author who had Mary Crawford joke in *Mansfield Park* that "Of *Rears*, and *Vices*, I saw enough," a pun about anal sex between men, was no shrinking violet. She could crack a bawdy remark of her own, too. Writing to her sister, Cassandra, about the family's upcoming move to Bath, she deadpanned that "we plan having a steady Cook, & a young giddy Housemaid, with a sedate, middle aged Man, who is to undertake the double office of Husband to the former & sweetheart to the latter.—No children of course to be allowed on either side." Of a woman who had just given birth for the eighteenth time, she told an unmarried niece, "I would recommend to her and Mr. D. the simple regimen of separate rooms." Elsewhere she remarked more seriously, of the figure of Don Juan, "I must say that I have seen nobody on the stage who has a more interesting Character than that compound of Cruelty & Lust."

If she didn't put sex in her novels, it wasn't because she was ignorant of it, or frightened of it, or because people didn't write such things in those days. In fact, they wrote them all the time. The books that she read as a teenager were ripe with lurid sexuality: abductions, seductions, cries, and caresses; bared

bosoms and eager kisses; cads and rakes and libertines; slaver-
ing monks and ravished maidens, callous bawds and poxy
whores; adultery, voyeurism, incest, and rape. If those kinds of
things were missing from her books, it was because she chose
to keep them out.

But they weren't completely missing. In *Mansfield Park,* a
married woman abandoned her husband to throw herself into
the arms of a lover. In *Pride and Prejudice,* a teenage girl was
seduced by a smiling deceiver. In *Sense and Sensibility,* Austen
gave us both scenarios: a young woman bore the child of an
adulterous affair, then that child, a generation later, was seduced, impregnated, and abandoned in turn. It was enough to
fill a novel—but not an Austen novel. That episode, like the two
in the other books, occurred offstage; in each case, we heard
of it only by report. Austen did not want to tell the kind of
story about young women that everyone else was telling. Her
heroines weren't passive, weren't piteous, weren't victims,
weren't playthings. They controlled their destinies; they stood
as equals.

In her age, that meant controlling their impulses, too. How
her ideas about sex might have changed in a world of reliable
birth control, no-fault divorce, and women's economic inde-
pendence we cannot say. It is certainly by no means clear that
she would have denounced the moral standards of today. But
that is really beside the point. She didn't condemn sexual im-
pulsiveness just because it could lead to ruin. She condemned
it because she thought it was a stupid reason to get married,
too. Her novels were stocked with intelligent men who'd made

the mistake of marrying vapid beauties and lived to regret it for the rest of their lives.

Mr. Bennet, in *Pride and Prejudice*—condemned to doing battle with his wife's eternal "nerves"—was one. Sir Thomas Bertram, in *Mansfield Park*—the proud possessor of a useless trophy wife—was another. In *Sense and Sensibility,* a certain Mr. Palmer made a third—having married a silly little dumpling with "a very pretty face" who "came in with a smile, smiled all the time of her visit, except when she laughed, and smiled when she went away," and whom her husband, only twenty-five or -six, had already made a habit of ignoring.

Somehow, though she died a virgin, Austen understood all this. For her heroes and heroines, sexual attraction was always the last thing, never the first. It didn't create affection, it flowed from it. Her heroines were usually not paragons of beauty. (If we think otherwise, that is, once again, because of the movies.) Anne Elliot, in *Persuasion,* was faded. Fanny Price, in *Mansfield Park,* was "not plain-looking." Catherine Morland, in *Northanger Abbey,* was "almost pretty." And Elizabeth Bennet, of course, was "tolerable, but not handsome enough to tempt *me.*" Other young ladies—Jane Bennet, Isabella Thorpe, Mary Crawford, Henrietta and Louisa Musgrove—often overshadowed them. But their looks grew on you, snuck up on you, as you got to know them, until one day you found yourself considering them, as someone finally said about Elizabeth, "one of the handsomest women of my acquaintance." As for Austen's heroes, they tended to the quiet, steady, sensitive type. It often took a while to be attracted to them, too. Her villains were the dashing ones, the flashy ones, the talkers and the flirters. She liked the kind of man who let his character speak for itself.

But none of this meant that her lovers—or her stories, or Austen herself—were passionless. If that was less obvious than many readers through the years have wanted it to be— Charlotte Brontë missing "what throbs fast and full," Mark Twain feeling "like a barkeep entering the kingdom of heaven"—it wasn't out of bloodlessness, but tact. Sir Walter Scott himself, in one of the earliest reviews of Austen's work, had lodged the same complaint. In *Emma,* he said, "Cupid walks decorously, and with good discretion, bearing his torch under a lanthorn [i.e., lantern], instead of flourishing it around to set the house on fire." The key word there, however, is "discretion." If Elinor refused to admit that what she felt for Edward was love, that was only because, unlike her histrionic sister, she wanted to preserve her privacy. Such feelings were too precious to violate by talking about.

Her creator felt the same. Of course her lovers were passionate—even Elinor and Edward, as I now saw: more deeply, more truly passionate than a butterfly like Willoughby could ever understand. All the more reason, then, to shield their intimacy from our prying eyes. The most remarkable thing about the love scenes with which her novels culminated, I realized— another thing the movies never stand for—was that she always turned away at the moment of truth. The hero was about to propose, the heroine was about to accept—their passion was about to be revealed at last—and Austen knew we wanted nothing more than to hear the words that sealed their happiness. And yet she always teasingly withheld them. "In what manner he expressed himself," we read in *Sense and Sensibility*, "and how he was received, need not be particularly told." "What did she say?" she asked of Emma. "Just what she ought, of course. A lady always does." It was too private; it was none of our business. And that was the most romantic thing of all.

What did that happiness consist of—the happiness her lovers achieved? The critic who said that friendship was "the true light of life" in Austen's view was only, I saw, half right. Friendship, he meant, as opposed to love. But for Austen, friendship was the very essence of love. However mad the statement made both Marianne and us, Elinor was onto something after all: "I do not attempt to deny that I think very highly of him—that I greatly esteem, that I like him." When I went back and looked at the other novels, I found the very same ideas. "She respected, she esteemed, she was grateful to him," I read of Elizabeth Bennet, "she felt a real interest in his welfare." "He is very good natured," said Emma's ditzy friend Harriet Smith, getting it wrong for the right reasons, "and I shall always feel much obliged to him, and have a great regard for—but that is quite a different thing from—." No, I finally saw, it's exactly the same.

If love begins in friendship, I was now able to see, it has to adhere to the principles of friendship as Austen understood them. The lover's highest role, like the friend's, is to help you to become a better person: push you, if necessary, even at the risk of wounded feelings. Austen's lovers challenged each other: to be less selfish, more aware, kinder, more considerate—not only toward each other but to everyone around them. Love, I

saw, for Austen—and what a change this was from the days of
my rebellious youth—is an agent not of subversion, but of so-
cialization. Lovers aren't supposed to goad each other toward
extremes of transgression, the way that Marianne and Willoughby did; they're supposed to teach each other the value of
behaving with propriety and decorum, show each other that
society's expectations are worthy, after all, of respect. Love, for
Austen, is not about remaining forever young. It's about becoming an adult.

Austen understood, even cherished, the passions of youth,
but she also knew that that is all they are. "There is something
so amiable in the prejudices of a young mind," said an older
character of Marianne, "that one is sorry to see them give way
to the reception of more general opinions." It's natural to believe the things that Marianne and I had believed about love,
but it's also necessary, if melancholy, to give them up. Austen
had respect for Elinor, but it was perfectly clear that the character she loved the most in *Sense and Sensibility* was her sister.
Yet just because she loved her so much, she loved her enough
to want to see her happy. And for Austen, as I already knew, the
key to happiness was letting life surprise you.

The only thing that's shocking about the way young lovers
act, I realized now, is how predictable it is. *Of course* Marianne
and Willoughby fell in love. It's what everyone knew they were
going to do; it was what *they* knew there were going to do, even
before they met each other. But making a mature decision, patiently feeling and thinking your way toward mutual respect and
regard and esteem, accepting the responsibility of challenging
and being challenged, refusing both the comforts of fantasy and

the cynicism of calculation—that is the really radical, the really original, the really heroic move. *That* is the true freedom; that is the way you lift yourself above the bondage of impulse and cliché. The marriages that ended Austen's novels, I now went back and saw, were always unexpected. Marianne and Willoughby were supposedly perfect for each other, but the men that Austen's heroines actually married were always the "wrong" person: the wrong class, the wrong age, the wrong temperament. Emma, Elizabeth, Anne—nobody around them saw their happiness coming. Not even, most importantly, themselves.

True love takes you by surprise, Austen was telling us, and if it's really worth something, it continues to take you by surprise. The last thing that lovers should do, despite what Marianne and I imagined, is agree about everything and share all of each other's tastes. True love, for Austen, means a never-ending clash of opinions and perspectives. If your lover's already just like you, then neither one of you has anywhere to go. Their character matters not only because you're going to have to live with it, but because it's going to shape the person *you* become.

For Charles Musgrove, who married Anne Elliot's whiny, trivial sister Mary in *Persuasion,* "a woman of real understanding might have given more consequence to his character, and more usefulness, rationality, and elegance to his habits and pursuits. As it was, he did nothing with much zeal but sport; and his time was otherwise trifled away." That was a quiet tragedy, but it was a tragedy nonetheless. With a better choice of mate, even John Dashwood, Elinor and Marianne's repulsive half brother, might well have been saved: "Had he married a more amiable woman, he might . . . have been made amiable himself;

for he was very young when he married, and very fond of his wife. But Mrs. John Dashwood was a strong caricature of himself;—more narrow-minded and selfish." "A strong caricature of himself": wanting to be with someone who's exactly like you, I now saw, isn't really love; it's only self-love. When Marianne finally did find a husband, Austen made sure to give her a man who was as different from her as possible.

And that was the most momentous revelation of all. Not only does your happiness depend upon your choice of mate, your very self depends upon it—your character, your soul. Love is more than just good feelings. A friction-free relationship, supposing that such a thing were even possible, would, I now saw, be a desert. Conflict is good, disagreements are good, even fights can be good. These were astounding new ideas to me. Committing yourself to someone doesn't have to limit your growth; it can be the door to perpetual growth. Austen had finally done what I never imagined possible. She had started to make me feel like getting married might not be such a terrible thing.

Yet there was still one lesson more for me to absorb. Of all of Austen's beliefs about love, the hardest one to accept was this: not everyone is capable of it. The evidence was overwhelming, once I was willing to face it. John Dashwood was not, his wife was not, and neither, I realized, were many other characters in Austen's books—most of the Elliots, in *Persuasion,* most of the Bertrams, in *Mansfield Park,* and lots of others everywhere:

the cold ones, the grasping ones, the ones who thought only of themselves. The essential requirement for love, in Austen's view—before the work, before the courage—is simply to possess a loving heart. And not everyone, she thought, is born with one of those.

That was what she meant when she assured her niece, while giving her romantic advice, "I do still think you *very* capable of being really in love." On hearing of Captain Benwick's second engagement in *Persuasion*, Anne Elliot thought, "He had an affectionate heart. He must love somebody." The disposition to love is the thing. If you have it, someone will come along to satisfy it. If you don't, it doesn't matter what happens. People can grow, Austen thought, but they can't fundamentally change.

By the same token, I now recognized, the great maker of fictional matches did not believe that most marriages work out very well. People marry for the wrong reasons, or they choose the wrong person, or circumstances are against them, or they just stop trying, or they aren't the kind of people who should marry in the first place. After a long, perilous process of maturation and mutual discovery, her heroes and heroines could look forward to a happy future, but of the unions her novels actually showed us (parents and neighbors and so on), the overwhelming number—something like sixteen out of twenty—were failures.

So where did that leave me? Austen reassured her niece, but what would she have said to me? Did I have a loving heart, or did all of my breakups, all of my bitterness, all of my failures to stay committed mean that I was one of those people who shouldn't even think of getting married? Maybe I had had the right idea from the start; maybe I'd been trying to tell myself something. After six years and six novels, these were the questions to which Jane Austen had brought me. But the answers, I knew, would not be found in any book.

There was one person, we can be sure, who did have a loving heart—Austen herself. That is the great question that hangs above her life. Not, how a person who never married could have known so much about love. The mysteries of genius are enough to explain that conundrum. But rather, why a person who knew so much about love, and had such a clear capacity for it, never did get married herself.

She might have been about to once, when she was Elizabeth Bennet's age. The record of Austen's letters opens like a novel. She is twenty, and writing to her sister in a rush of high spirits about the ball she has gone to the night before:

> *Mr. H. began with Elizabeth, and afterwards danced with her again; but* they *do not know* how to be particular. *I flatter myself, however, that they will profit by the three successive lessons which I have given them. You scold me so much in the nice long letter which I have this moment received from you, that I am almost afraid to tell you how my Irish friend and I behaved. Imagine to yourself everything most profligate and shocking in the way of dancing and sitting down together. I can* expose myself, *however,* only *once more, because he leaves the country soon after next Friday,*

on which day we are to have a dance at Ashe after all. He is a very gentlemanlike, good-looking, pleasant young man, I assure you. But as to our having ever met, except at the three last balls, I cannot say much; for he is so excessively laughed at about me at Ashe, that he is ashamed of coming to Steventon, and ran away when we called on Mrs. Lefroy a few days ago.

"My Irish friend" was Tom Lefroy, nephew of Anne Lefroy, Austen's beloved older friend and surrogate mother, on a Christmas visit to his cousins at their home at Ashe, a couple of miles from the Austens' place at Steventon. (Tom's father had settled in Ireland as a young man.) Their romance evidently flared up very quickly. Three evenings were enough— three evenings of dancing and flirting and talking, of hopes and glances and laughter—to seal their mutual attachment. Six days later, the day before the ball at Ashe, Austen wrote to her sister again:

Tell Mary that I make over Mr. Heartley & all his Estate to her for her sole use and Benefit in future, & not only him, but all my other Admirers into the bargain wherever she can find them, even the kiss which C. Powlett wanted to give me, as I mean to confine myself in future to Mr. Tom Lefroy, for whom I do not care sixpence.

The feeling, as always, was hedged by a laugh, but it was no less in earnest for that. The moment of truth, Austen felt sure, was about to arrive. "I look forward with great impatience to it," she said of the next day's ball, "as I rather expect to receive an offer from my friend in the course of the evening." Yes, an offer—a proposal.

And yet it was not to be. We do not know what happened that night—the record of Austen's letters breaks off at that point (Cassandra burned everything she deemed too sensitive), and the next one dates from the following summer. But we do know that Tom's family took stock of the situation and decided to put a stop to it. Tom was the oldest son of a large and by no means wealthy family. He was studying for the bar and still making his way in the world, and he could not afford to engage himself, or so it was thought, to a fortuneless young woman. As his cousins later said, their mother sent him off posthaste so "that no more mischief might be done."

Would he have proposed, as Austen expected, had he not been interfered with? We cannot know. Did he return her love in equal measure? Of that we can be sure. Decades later, as an old man—he had married (an heiress) three years later, fathered nine children, and risen to become Lord Chief Justice of Ireland—"he said in so many words," according to a nephew, "that he was in love with her, although he qualified his confession by saying it was a boyish love." A boyish love it may have been, at least from the perspective of old age, but twenty-one years after their brief romance—the only time they ever met— he had traveled back to England (no small journey) to pay his respects after learning of her death. Still later he had bought, at an auction of the publisher's papers, the rejection letter that Austen had received for the first version of *Pride and Prejudice*. His feelings, it seemed, had never died.

As for Austen's, it is harder to say. His only other mention in her letters came almost three years after that fateful Christmas season. Anne Lefroy, his aunt, had just been visiting, and, Austen reported:

> *I was enough alone to hear all that was interesting, which you will easily credit when I tell you that of her nephew she said nothing at all, and of her friend* [another young man] *very little. She did not once mention the name of the former to me, and I was too proud to make any enquiries; but on my father's afterwards asking where he was, I learnt that he was going back to London in his way to Ireland, where he is called to the Bar and means to practise.*

The tone is unmistakable: lingering resentment, continued curiosity, and yet, as well, a sense that she has gotten over it. Tom Lefroy had taught her what it meant to be in love, but Austen was no Anne Elliot, pining away for Wentworth. It was not disappointment that made her a spinster.

For one thing, there were other opportunities. Austen was, by all accounts, an attractive young woman: tall and slender, with bright hazel eyes; long, curly, light brown hair; a clear and glowing complexion; and a light, firm step that spoke of health and animation. Of her charms of conversation, her playfulness and wit, there can be, of course, no doubt. Tom Lefroy was hardly the only young man to be drawn to her. There was "Mr. Heartley & all his Estate," and Charles Powlett, who wanted to kiss her, and who knows how many other "Admirers." After Tom there was that friend of Anne Lefroy's, the one that Austen mentioned in the letter three years later, a young clergyman who had expressed regard and interest. There was a young gentleman in a seaside place—the details are as hazy as the setting, for Cassandra divulged the episode only years after her sister's death—"whose charm of person, mind, and manners," according to a nephew, "was such that Cassandra thought him worthy to possess and likely to win her sister's love," who took his leave "expressing his intention of soon seeing them again"— but who, a short time later, suddenly died. And then, of course, there was Harris Bigg-Wither.

Could Austen have grown to love her fiancé-for-a-night, as she later advised her niece to do with John Plumptre? Perhaps. She had known him since childhood, she loved his family, and although he was still somewhat shy and awkward, he had come back from Oxford a far more confident young man than he had once been. But love was no longer the only consideration. The young woman who had lost her chance with Tom Lefroy at the age of twenty had still been only a fledgling writer. The one who rejected her friends' brother seven years later was now the author of three novels, even if none were published yet. She had come to a fork in the road. In one direction lay marriage, family, security, and perhaps love. In the other lay the adventure of art.

She could not have had both. To marry then, for a young woman, was to become a mother to the exclusion of all else— and at the cost, finally, far too often, of life. Austen's brother Charles's wife had four children in five years and died. Austen's brother Frank's wife had eleven children in sixteen years and

died. Austen's brother Edward's wife had eleven children in fifteen years and died. Austen's mother had had eight children.
When Austen thought about the fact that her favorite niece
would someday find a husband—this was several years after the
John Plumptre episode—she feared for what it would mean.
"Oh! what a loss it will be, when you are married," she exclaimed, telling us everything we need to know about why she
never got married herself: "I shall hate you when your delicious
play of Mind is all settled down into conjugal & maternal affections." Cassandra would later remember the letters her sister
wrote, "triumphing over the married women of her acquaintance, and rejoicing in her own freedom"—the freedom to write,
the freedom to create, the freedom to ride her incomparable
genius wherever it wanted to go.

That freedom would be tragically cut short. The worst irony
of Austen's death at the age of forty-one, young even for those
days, was that she came from a remarkably long-lived family.
Of her parents and seven siblings, eight lived past seventy. Cassandra lived to seventy-two. Their mother lived to eighty-seven.
Their brother Frank, the sailor, lived to ninety-one, rising to the
highest rank in the Royal Navy. The cause of Austen's untimely
demise will never be known. Scholars once suspected that the
fatal illness was Addison's disease, but a closer look at the evidence discredited the theory. Perhaps, if the cause was infection
or some other circumstantial factor, a different life—a life lived
in Ireland with Tom Lefroy, or on his estate with Harris Bigg-
Wither—might well have been a longer one.

A longer one, but a different one. Austen never married, but
she did have children, and many more than eight or eleven.

Their names are Emma and Elizabeth and Catherine, Anne and Fanny and Elinor and Marianne. Their names are Henry and Edward and Wentworth and Willoughby, Mr. Collins and Miss Bates and Mr. Darcy. They were not long-lived, they are ageless. Had she married Tom or Harris, she might have been happy, she might have been rich, she might have been a mother, she might have even been long-lived herself. She might have been all of these things—but we would not have been who we are, and she would not have been Jane Austen.

CHAPTER 7

the end of the story

It was early in September of my fourth year in Brooklyn. I was halfway through the third and final chapter of my dissertation and had just gone back to teaching. Meanwhile, my friend from Connecticut, the one who had fallen in love the previous year, was already getting ready for his wedding. The big event was planned for November, but he and his fiancée threw a party at their new house the weekend after Labor Day, so all their friends could get to know each other in advance.

His fiancée had grown up in Cleveland, and her best friend from home—like Austen and Martha Lloyd, the woman who shared her house, they were practically sisters—was going to be driving out for the festivities. I had heard that she was coming, and that she was single, but we didn't hit it off at first. They were playing Sinatra when I showed up, and even though I liked Sinatra, I tried to make an entrance with a snarky comment ("Can we please put on something a little less farty?") that—shades of Darcy and Elizabeth—only succeeded in making her think me a jerk.

We took our separate paths into the depths of the party, and I had all but forgotten about her a couple of hours later when I found us entangled, out of nowhere—another *Pride and Prejudice* moment—in the midst of an intricate, impassioned conversation. The subject was political; like an Austen heroine, I later discovered, she was testing to see if I had the right values. Slowly, as we stood there hashing it out, it began to dawn on me that the woman I had scarcely glanced at when I came in—I didn't know how I had managed to miss this—was, as Mr. Darcy put it, one of the handsomest women of my acquaintance. Not just beautiful, in other words, but attractive in a deeply compelling way.

Before the night was out, we were both completely hooked. I stayed for the rest of the weekend, then found myself devastated when we had to say good-bye. But neither one of us was going to let it go. We were five hundred miles apart, but before we knew it we were on the phone for hours at a time, doing exactly what Austen would have wanted us to do: learning about each other, and respecting each other, by listening to each other's stories.

We talked about our families, painted pictures of our lives, explored our thoughts about everything under the sun. I was paying attention not only to what she had to say, but also to the way that she expressed herself in saying it. The technology may have been updated for the twentieth century, but otherwise it

was exactly the same thing that had happened between Elinor
and Edward, and all of Austen's other heroes and heroines,
too. I was discovering the temper of this woman's heart and
mind—her "sentiments" and "opinions," her "imagination"
and "observation" and "taste"—and she was doing the same
with me. We were developing that mutual regard and esteem
that comes from knowledge of a person's character, not body.
The latter we already had—we hadn't just talked, that
weekend—but this was every bit as intimate. In fact, unlike
Austen's young people, we couldn't even see each other. It was
a completely disembodied experience: just two voices meeting
in the night, a conversation of souls, a separate little privacy
that only we inhabited.

"I'm crazy about her!" I told my friend's fiancée.

"Keep it together," she said. "I know she likes you, but if you
come on too strong, you'll scare her off."

I kept it together, but it was tough. The woman I had met
that weekend, I discovered as we whispered in each other's ears
on all those nights, was brilliant, articulate, intuitive, and stun-
ningly insightful. She knew how to talk, and she also knew how
to listen. She was cerebral without self-importance, sophisticated without pretension. She had a wicked sense of humor,
too, one that Austen would have certainly enjoyed. I told her
about someone I once knew who prided himself on his supposedly large vocabulary but who hadn't known the difference between "impotent" and "indolent," because he didn't know what
either one of them meant. "I know the difference," she shot
back. "Can't and won't."

She was also very different than me, more so than anyone I had ever been involved with. She had grown up middle-class, but she didn't have an expensive education and wasn't on her way to being a professional. She waited tables, like the woman I'd been seeing when I first read Austen and for whom I had had so little respect. She had been a shoeshine girl, had clerked at a record store, and was still slowly finishing her degree at a local public college as she worked full time. What's more, she had spent time with the kinds of people who I, with my sheltered elitist existence, had scarcely ever even talked to: working-class kids, art-school types, punk rockers, street people, old hippies.

The little Ivy League voice inside my head, which I had gotten from my family, was frantic about how unprestigious this all sounded. The little New York voice, which I had gotten from those fancy friends as well as from my general environment, had contempt for how unimpressive it looked. But I had read *Emma,* and knew that books were not the only way to learn, and I had read *Mansfield Park,* and knew that status and "success," so called, did not make a person valuable, and I didn't listen to those voices anymore. I had learned the lessons of Austen's love stories, and I understood that you should be with someone who isn't just your mirror image, someone you didn't see coming, someone who takes you beyond yourself. On just the other side of all those petty fears, I sensed the promise of immense possibilities.

About a month after that initial weekend, she drove out to Brooklyn to see if we really wanted to keep the relationship going, given how completely inconvenient it was. And what we discovered, as we each tried to figure out whether the other person was someone we could fall in love with, was that we already had. It had been coming on so gradually, as Elizabeth Bennet would have put it, that we hardly knew when it began.

The city never seemed so sweet to me as it did that fall. As I walked along the familiar streets, now utterly transformed, I bore my love for her about with me like an invisible crown. I'd thought I knew what love was meant to feel like, but I realized I hadn't had a clue. It had always been a thing that I could feel inside me, yet now it seemed like it was everywhere, filling everything, an atmosphere I moved within. I'd also always thought that relationships were something that you chose to have. But I hadn't chosen this one; it had chosen me. The question of whether I had a loving heart had answered itself.

It wasn't all smooth sailing, though. There were fights—of course there were. Neither one of us was perfect, certainly not me. When something came up, I still dug my trenches like anyone else. But what saved me, at those times, were two things that I had learned from Austen: that my girlfriend's perspective was just as valid as mine, however much it killed me in the middle of an argument to acknowledge it, and that if I had done something wrong, then allowing myself to recognize as much—no matter how awful it was to admit it, no matter how humiliating it was to have to lose a fight in which I had invested so much ego—was ultimately going to be good for me.

There would come a moment, after the minutes or the hours of conflict, in the middle of the hard words, when I would catch a glimpse, just a tiny glimpse, not just of the fact that I owed my girlfriend the apology that I knew I'd have to rake up my guts to give her, but that if I managed to cross that burning bridge, there would be something in it for me. I would learn; I would grow. I wouldn't have to make the same mistake again. I could be a better partner to her in the future, and a better person myself. That glimpse, that was the rope that was lowered into my cave; that was what enabled me to climb back out to sanity and love. And on her side, it was just the same. She helped me learn to say I'm sorry, and she helped me teach her, too.

That winter, I took her down to Mexico for a kind of relationship honeymoon. She'd told me how she'd loved the beach vacations that she'd taken as a girl, so I decided to surprise her with something extravagant. We went down to a little cabana place on an island near Cancún, where we spent the week lying on the beach like a pair of lizards, wandering the village streets, and racing mopeds along the back roads.

As winter turned into spring, our phone calls began to take on the structure of dates. We'd start by pouring ourselves drinks and catching each other up on the previous couple of days' worth of news. I'd sit out on the fire escape as the weather got warmer, the smell of lilac wafting up from the yards below. Then we'd each make dinner, sharing jokes and stories all the while, then keep talking far into the night, until we were literally falling asleep in midsentence.

When summer came, I went to stay with her in Cleveland. Some of my New York acquaintances were a little appalled that I was involved with someone who lived in the Midwest. One, that glamorous woman who had broken up with the guy from Ohio because he didn't dress well enough, ran into me one night. "Are you still going out with that girl from St. *Louis*?" she demanded. When I introduced my girlfriend to another one of those people, the son of a fairly well-known modern artist, he said, "Oh, *I've* been to Cincinnati. I thought it was just going to be a bunch of strip malls. But you know, it wasn't really that bad."

No, Cleveland (at least *I* knew the difference) wasn't bad at all. There's life, I discovered, outside New York. In fact, with the way my girlfriend made it come alive for me, I came to sort of love the place. As we drove and walked the neighborhoods and streets, she peeled back the layers of memory for me— showed me her old houses and old haunts, gave me the backstories, introduced me to the people she'd been telling me about. She was retracing her life, and weaving me into it.

I set up my computer in her living room and started hammering out the introduction to my dissertation, the last piece left. I turned her on to Leonard Cohen, with whom I'd been obsessed since the darkest days of my depression, and she taught me how to drink martinis. I hid about a half dozen presents all over the apartment on her birthday that July, and she baked me fortune cookies with naughty messages inside. Of course, my little gray cat had come with me for the summer—she would curl up on the pillow between us—and when I went back to Brooklyn at the end of August, I left her in my girlfriend's care, to keep a little piece of me with her.

It wasn't long before they both were back. By the end of the year, my girlfriend had packed up and moved in with me. Now my city became hers, too. We ate black bean cakes in Chinatown, blini in Brighton Beach, and bowls of flaczki at Christine's. We watched the Brooklyn Bridge at sunset from the railing of the Promenade. The owner of a shop in Little Italy helped us toast our relationship with tiny cups of fifty-year-old balsamic vinegar that he pulled out from the back of the store, as thick and sweet as maple syrup.

It was all falling together. She was by my side when I finally finished my dissertation that spring, and she was there when, miracle of miracles, I actually landed a job. It was even in Connecticut. We were going to be joining the circle of friends, the substitute family, through whom we had found each other.

And all the while, she had been meeting the important people in my life. She met my parents—the first time I had ever brought anyone home—who seemed to have trouble believing that their baby boy (I was thirty-three by that point) was finally growing up. She met my professor, who had us over for dinner and treated us like equals. She met the couple who had introduced me to the high-society crowd, who didn't get her at all. And she became acquainted with my best friend, who really did know me better than I knew myself, because she welcomed her as the partner I had always been searching for.

.   .   .

That first weekend she came to Brooklyn, the visit that sealed
our fate, she brought along a book, just in case there was some
downtime. She knew I was a graduate student by that point,
but she had no idea what I studied or whom I was writing my
dissertation about. It was just the thing she happened to be
reading at the time.

The book was *Pride and Prejudice.*

Reader, I married her.

acknowledgments

My first thanks go to my agent, Elyse Cheney, who encouraged me to undertake this project and provided invaluable, unstinting guidance in shaping it. Gratitude also to my editor, Ann Godoff, for giving me the freedom to find my voice, and to the staffs at Cheney Literary and Penguin Press, for all their creativity and care. Thanks as well to the friends who believed in the book along the way and who helped me believe in it, too. Two volumes were indispensable: Claire Tomalin's biography and Deirdre Le Faye's edition of the letters. My highest thanks go to Karl Kroeber, who started it all, and to Aleeza Jill Nussbaum, who gave me the perfect ending.